SPEAKING THE TRUTH

More Praise for
Speaking the Truth

"Sam Wells's sermons are not simple, but they are direct—from the heart of Scripture to the hearts of his American audience. With compassion, imagination, gentle humor, and breathtaking intelligence, he helps us to view our culture and ourselves from the one perspective that is genuinely fresh: the perspective of eternity."

Ellen F. Davis, Professor of Bible and Practical Theology, Duke Divinity School

"These bracing sermons, as pastorally and politically practical as they are deeply theological, are among the finest I have read. Wells's spoken truth fairly (but winsomely) slaps us in the face to snap the church in America out of its power-and-privilege-induced stupor and seeks to awaken it (for a third time?) to the urgent task of listening for and responding to the heart of God in the word of God. An exemplary display of public speaking by a pastor-theologian that transcends the traditional conservative/liberal labels."

Kevin J. Vanhoozer, Research Professor of Systematic Theology, Trinity Evangelical Divinity School

SPEAKING THE TRUTH

Preaching in a Pluralistic Culture

Samuel Wells

Abingdon Press
Nashville

Library of Congress Cataloging-in-Publication Data

Wells, Samuel, 1965-
   Speaking the truth: preaching in a pluralistic culture / Samuel Wells.
      p. cm.
   ISBN 978-0-687-64689-0 (binding: pbk., adhesive perfect binding : alk. paper)
   1. Sermons, American—21st century. 2. Universities and colleges—Sermons. I. Title.

BV4310.W38 2008
252'.03—dc22

                                                                              2008024596

08 09 10 11 12 13 14 15 16 17—10 9 8 7 6 5 4 3 2 1
MANUFACTURED IN THE UNITED STATES OF AMERICA

To John Inge

Contents

Preface

I was installed as Dean of Duke Chapel by the president of the university with the words, "Be among us as one who speaks the truth." Each word of the phrase "speaking the truth" is worth pondering.

The heart of this book lies in the ambivalence of the word *truth*. On the one hand it means an ingenuous, candid, thoughtful interjection of sometimes uncomfortable, disruptive, and disconcerting but nonetheless life-giving wisdom. The boy says to the emperor: "You have no clothes"; the prophet says to David: "You are the man." In a culture of sophistication and ambition, the truth is a word of simplicity and transparency. But on the other hand, when spoken within the church, *truth* means Christ, the image of the invisible God. Speaking the truth means perceiving how the transformation brought about in Christ permeates and overturns every detail of human existence. This is truth with a capital *T*.

If contemporary culture is skeptical about the word *truth*, it is even more deeply suspicious about the word *the*. For much of the church's history and for much of American history, the word *the* has been brought into disrepute by people who spoke of "the truth" and meanwhile backed it up by force of arms or methods of social control. This book is written in the conviction that the church is better off without the forms of social control but should not give up on the word *the*. In my introduction, I narrate how the social control and the *the* came to seem inseparable, but it may be that only in a church with fewer evidences of social influence can the word *the* once again come to be used without reserve. The claims about Jesus really do redescribe the world, but when spoken from a location of obvious social advantage, they become very hard to hear.

For all the misgivings in university culture about *the* and *truth*, *speaking* is still in fashion. My principal role at Duke is to ensure that, on the many occasions I have the opportunity to speak to very large numbers of people, I have something to say. There is an irony in my role because one gains a reputation as a *preacher* because (presumably) one is thought to have something to say about Jesus, but as a *speaker* one is frequently asked to refrain from identifying Jesus as the source of one's reflections. Colleges and universities in America affirm and assert their identity at grand public occasions such as convocations and baccalaureates. Such occasions are marked by two contrasting characteristics. One is a sense of expectation that the speaker or speakers will capture the significance of the moment and place it in the larger context of the lives of the university, its members, its values, and the wider culture. Another is a sense of suspicion that any speaker is coming from a particular social location and, particularly if the speaker holds a religious (often Christian) office like I do, that their words doubtless have little to offer a culture of plural spirituality. This tension creates a paradox: Something Must Be Said—but nothing can be. This volume strives to offer theory and example to explore the nature of that tension and to propose some paths through it.

This book is designed to be read in three ways. It is, first, an assessment of the current and historical aspects that make Christianity in America distinctive, as seen through the eyes of a relative newcomer from Europe. The introduction identifies the challenge and the opportunity of being part of the church, particularly in a research university setting, in the United States today. In that sense the rest of the book offers examples of how to address the context outlined in the introduction.

The book is, second, a series of ad hoc attempts to name the activity of the Holy Spirit in the life of a particular community over the course of two years. The material in this book falls fairly neatly into seven themes, but each address arose in response to the needs and events of a moment in time that was both unique— in the sense that every moment is—and very ordinary. In this sense, each section of each chapter stands alone in its own right, and the other material in each chapter and the introduction to the book merely provide a commentary to the direct words of the occasion.

Finally the book is, third, a recognition that the Duke Chapel pulpit is a highly visible one and that those who occupy it regularly have a duty not only to pay attention to the way their words will be heard but also to make their approach available for imitation. For this reason, each sermon is prefaced by some words of introduction to set the scene and to invite the reader to share in the theological, exegetical, and rhetorical issues being evaluated as the sermon took shape.

Duke University at its best is a young institution energized and inspired by high standards, high ideals, and no fear. Duke Chapel at its best is an institution seeking to harmonize a generous but orthodox quest for truth and a compassionate and profound longing for justice, each focused on a detailed and exuberant attention to worship. Duke Divinity School at its best articulates, practices, and teaches the ethos of what, in my introduction, I describe as "chapter three." America at its best combines energy, excellence, compassion, justice, beauty, and faith. But I hope my attempts to engage the culture in which I live will have something to offer those who have little specific knowledge or interest in Duke University, its chapel, its divinity school, or even America.

In the past, I seldom wrote sermons down. I always thought, *If I want my congregation to remember what I've said, I should be able to remember what I've said.* Since I started preaching at Duke Chapel, I have invariably written sermons down. It's partly because I'm still getting used to speaking to a thousand people on a regular basis, and it would be a little awkward if I forgot what I was going to say. It's partly because I work as part of a wonderful team, and the liturgy is greatly enhanced if my colleagues know what's coming from the pulpit and I can give them a copy a few days out to prepare their spoken, musical, and other contributions. But it's mostly because I have learned that countless people interact with the sermons in written form. They provoke and catalyze and facilitate playful and earnest conversations between people of assured faith, troubled faith, and no faith; between students, faculty, and staff; between physicians and their patients; attorneys and their partners; postal workers and residents; housekeepers and tourists. Finally, it is in encouraging such conversations, and in enjoying the Spirit's work in them, that I have come to understand the value of written sermons.

The privilege of preaching to a large and thoughtful congregation in a beautiful setting supported by magnificent music is more than matched by the company of ministers and musicians with whom every detail of worship is cherished and enhanced. I am profoundly grateful for Craig Kocher, with whom I have shared the profoundest heart-searchings over what to say in times of crisis, tragedy, and sorrow. I am likewise blessed to minister alongside people like Rodney Wynkoop, David Arcus, Allan Friedman, and Bob Parkins, who are called musicians but whose excellence in music is matched by their compassion and courage as pastors. I have shared as well as received the ministry of Nancy Ferree-Clark, Keith Daniel, Gaston Warner, Abby Kocher, and Meghan Feldmeyer, and each has touched me deeply.

I am honored by the friendships of those who tell me when I'm wrong and show me where to find the truth. Conversations and wonderings with Stanley Hauerwas, Greg Jones, Richard Brodhead, and John Kiess have pervaded the arguments of this volume. I have had the privilege of coming to know some of the American church's greatest exegetes and preachers, including Ched Myers, Walter Brueggeman, Ellen Davis, and Richard Hays, and to call such people my friends. I have been enriched by attentive listeners—and thoughtful critics—including Lucy Worth, John Sharon, Ana Ponce, Judy Hays, Neville Black, Ira Mueller, Jim Kelly, Marty Gagliano, Bruce Mueller, Oscar Dantzler, Dwayne Huebner, and Dick White. And I have been blessed to wrestle with those who are not Christians but who challenge me to work out what being a Christian means, especially Noah Pickus and Michael Goldman.

Among those who have asked me questions to which I didn't know the answer, I am especially appreciative of Trygve Johnson, Elizabeth Kiss, and Brent Waters. They pushed me to articulate the arguments that form the introduction to this book. Among those who helped me envisage this project is Ben Wayman, whose enthusiasm, thoughtfulness, and friendship have made shaping this book such a pleasure. Mandie Manring and Jackie Andrews have faithfully made most of these words available to many enquirers. And David Warbrick, Jenny Warbrick, and Rebekah Eklund have gently assisted me in reading the material through the eyes of the church.

The best sermon is a life well lived, and the finest liturgy is the daily rhythm of need, thanksgiving, forgiveness, and joy. For these, in awe and admiration, my deepest thanks are to my wife, Jo.

The book is dedicated to John Inge, teacher, pastor, preacher, friend, who has shown me what it means to speak the truth.

Introduction

Speaking the Truth in America

The Three-chapter Story

Behind the tensions in modern American higher education lies a story. It's a story that's widely accepted in university and college circles—so widely, in fact, that it's seldom articulated. The story takes place in three chapters with a prologue. The prologue we could call prehistory. Prehistory was a time before 1900. In prehistory, there were colleges and universities founded, shaped, and dominated by the major Christian traditions.[1] There were, no doubt, struggles over a whole host of scholarly and ecclesial principles—but in general this period is remembered about as clearly as the time of the dinosaurs and is considered just as relevant.

History really begins in chapter one, which broadly covers the first half of the twentieth century. Chapter one names the period when the churches traded their theological identity in order to retain their institutional influence. Faculties in many, perhaps most, of the church-related colleges and universities wrested control of those institutions away from the ecclesial hierarchies. Most of the tussles about academic freedom and such litmus tests as the teaching of evolution went the way of the faculties. The period was experienced by many as a time of conflict over scholarship and college culture, but it is *remembered* as a period when the stranglehold of white Anglo-Saxon control was tightened and the consensus among the dominant churches, institutions, and social groups was overwhelming. It was experienced by many as a time of economic hardship, but it is *remembered* as a period of social privilege because particular social classes enjoyed access to opportunities from which others were excluded.

Chapter two refers to the period of significant social change largely associated with the third quarter of the last century. The

1

way the story is remembered, excluded groups, notably African Americans and women, beat down the doors of segregation and restricted access. White Anglo-Saxon males stopped being seen as the source of all good and started being fingered as the cause of all evil. All this was against the backdrop of the Cold War, the Vietnam period, and the sexual revolution. This period, known as "the dying of the light," was characterized by a host of converging and diverging forces.[2] Those inclined or tempted to follow a secularization hypothesis see chapter two as a more or less inevitable disenchantment of the world with its religious metanarratives. Seen as a power struggle, the issue was not inherently about religious truth or plausibility at all. For example, the widespread assumption that chapter two renders Christian identity problematic in a campus context tends to ignore the depth to which the motivation and inspiration of many African Americans at the heart of the liberation movements were rooted in that same Christian tradition. Chapter two is remembered less as a process of secularization and more as a revolt against privilege and hierarchy of any kind, as well as a statement of a profound confidence in the untrammeled will of the individual when given free expression.

The purpose of telling this three-chapter story is to suggest that chapter two is not an end point and that American colleges and universities now find themselves in a new context, which I am calling chapter three. Chapter three is often portrayed as a battleground. On the one hand are those who identify strongly with the spirit of chapter two. On the other hand are those who lament all that they feel was lost in the passing of chapter one. It is this battleground that makes the identification of this three-chapter narrative so significant, and it is this battleground that makes it evident how widespread and largely unquestioned is the assumption of its broad outline. The problem is that chapter three as yet does not seem to have an undisputed narrative of its own. Those focused on the poverty of the two-thirds world, global warming, AIDS, or the so-called war on terror may be inclined to regard chapter three as characterized by crisis; others see the current American student generation as inebriated by affluence and lacking either the passion of the previous chapter or the earnest purpose of the first chapter.

Those who have an interest in the advanced study and teaching of religion in general and Christianity in particular will recognize how this story has been played out in seminaries, divinity schools, and religion departments. In many establishments, the religion department or divinity school was an inherently chapter-one institution. The story assumed that Protestant Christianity was the template in relation to which all other forms of religious expression would be evaluated. Chapter two names the period when religious studies began to assert itself as the new paradigm. No longer was Christianity or any other faith to be best understood from within Christianity. Now the best place to understand and assess faith was from outside faith, at least procedurally if not existentially. The role of theology in the university seemed, to many, to be problematic, not perhaps because theology's fruits had been barren and its methods moribund but rather because it seemed to epitomize the spirit of chapter one.

In his novel *How Far Can You Go?* the Roman Catholic writer David Lodge charts the effect of the social changes of what I am calling chapter two on a series of characters coming of age in the England of the period. Commenting on one couple who were a little slow to wake up to the new mores of the 1970s, Lodge says, they "were having their sixties a little late."[3] The same could broadly be said of the American church in relation to the three-chapter story I have been telling. The American church in many ways has been a chapter behind the university.[4] There is no doubt that chapter three does not describe the whole of the American higher education scene today, and it certainly does not describe the whole of the American church scene. There are places where chapters two and one—and even the prologue—are still visible, significant, or even dominant aspects of the narrative. When one travels across a variety of American campuses and to a variety of American churches one finds not only institutions and individuals who are living in chapter one as if there never had been a chapter two but also institutions and individuals who are fighting in chapter two as if there were no chapter three. Needless to say, there is considerable heterogeneity in each chapter. There have always been people living a chapter three ethos, even when the dominant narrative was of another chapter, just as there are very many people living today as if there were no chapter three. For example, aspects of the early civil rights movement would, I suspect, have felt much more at home in chapter three than in chapter two. The usefulness of the three-chapter story is not to tidy individuals and movements neatly into one quasi-historical chapter or another but rather to identify a narrative that has a powerful hold on the contemporary imagination and to locate the unique opportunity it presents for the American church today.

My judgment is that in the popular American imagination the narrative of the prologue, chapter one, and chapter two is largely beyond dispute. Each period of course has its areas of modest controversy. For some, the prologue is not irrelevant at all but is a period to be revisited for vision and purpose to back up the institutional memory of the first chapter or the liberating longing of the second. For others, chapter one is wrongly characterized as a period of privilege but should be described as a period of hardship and struggle. For others again, there is a dispute over whether chapter two is inherently non- or anti-religious, or whether it is incomprehensible without religious conviction. Many people in America have had little or no exposure to any form of Christianity that is not obsessed by the aspirations of chapter one, and they often assume that chapter two has thus discredited the whole premise of the church. But the real issue is none of the above. The real issue is that the American university and the American church are now in chapter three, like it or not. And it is true that many people do not like it. Many people believe they must do everything they can to restore chapter one, and many other people are strongly invested in arguing that chapter two is still going on.

I propose that chapter three name the context and the agenda for exploring the context of the church in America today. While the church in other nations may not have had quite such the same three-chapter narrative, there are many nations where the churches can identify with what I am calling the third chapter.[5] This book is concerned with what it might mean to speak the truth in chapter three.

The Prologue and Its Double Legacy

Prophetic is a much-used word in the American church.[6] In the language I have been using, *prophetic* invariably means "in continuity with the tradition of chapter two." What the word reveals is a very particular reading of history. This reading of history makes two core assumptions. The first is that it is possible to skip chapter one and look back to what I have called the prologue and there find, in the original purposes of America, all the principles and values one could need to resource the vision of chapter two. Thus chapter two is not simply looking forward to a new dawn of liberation and the untrammeled expression of the inner good of each individual; it is at least as much looking back to the founding DNA of the nation, located in the Declaration of Independence and the Constitution. The second core assumption is that there is a special affinity between this period that I have called the prologue and the prophetic tradition of the Old Testament. Both scriptural Israel and historic America have a special place in God's heart. Both came to birth in escape from oppression. Both find their soul when they recall the way God provided for them through such fearful times. Both find their destiny as a light to other nations of the social harmony God has in store. And thus the prophetic tradition, when it demands equality for marginalized social groups and calls for those in conditions analogous to slavery to be set free, identifies not just with the founders of America but with the scriptural founders of Israel.[7]

Prophecy means placing an individual, an institution, or a situation in the light of a greater story. In the American context, prophecy has tended to mean recalling that all people have been made in God's image and are thus equal; that a particular people, first Israel, now America, has been called into a covenant relationship with God; that as for Israel so for America this covenant is jeopardized most acutely by the people's faulty memory; and that that faulty memory is most damagingly expressed in institutional oppression of the contemporary equivalent of the stranger, widow, and orphan—that is, those excluded by false barriers of class, race, or gender.

Prophecy thus has a quality in America significantly different from that found elsewhere because it is telling a story it assumes its listeners already know. It finds its power precisely in reinvigorating a story that has grown dusty through lack of use. But prophecy is scarcely possible if no story is commonly acknowledged as authoritative. In America the story has never grown dusty. This common story gives prophecy in America its unique quality. Moses led his people out of slavery, received the law, yet died before entering the Promised Land. The eighth-century prophets pleaded for Israel to recall its duty to the poor and outcast and thus to remember the story of its covenant with God—but they failed, and the northern kingdom was obliterated by the Assyrians. The founding fathers, like Moses, brought America to freedom and laid down the quasi-divine covenant with the people. Martin Luther King, Jr, like the eight-century prophets, pleaded with the nation to recall its foundation but, like Moses, died before reaching the Promised Land. These broad outlines of the story the prophet assumes everybody knows. The problem prophecy addresses is not so much evil, not so much an inherent flaw in the story, as forgetfulness of the prologue and its contemporary significance.

If chapter two presupposes a particular reading of the prologue, then so, in a different way, does chapter one. If chapter two could be characterized as prophecy, chapter one might be named responsibility. Responsibility names the desire of Christians to legislate the kingdom of God. Again in America the attraction of this social strategy rests on a particular reading of American history. Instead of assuming the prologue focuses on the period following the Declaration of Independence, this view looks back a century earlier to the Puritan hegemony in New England and to the Calvinist tradition of seeking a godly society. Like prophecy, it too looks to the Old Testament for its inspiration and validation, but its role models are not so much the prophets as the kings. Saul, David, and Solomon embody the kingly aspiration to see a person of God at the head of the affairs of state.

The much-cited first amendment to the Constitution is no barrier to the practice, or certainly the desire, of Christians to enforce conformity to what they perceive as Christian norms from people who are not Christians and have no desire to be. What should be an offer, an encouragement, a gift, becomes an expectation, an assumption, a requirement. Contemporary advocates of chapter one absorb the first amendment in much the same way as they absorb the legacy of chapter two: these are corrections to an otherwise seamless story.[8]

The problem with the seamless story goes further than the prophetic critique offered by the voice of chapter two, the cry of those excluded from the narrative. The problem is a theological one. It has two symptoms with one cause. The first symptom is that the church becomes invisible in both responsibility and prophecy modes. The scriptural archetypes assumed by both approaches are invariably Old Testament ones. The aspirations focus on the nation called out from among the nations, rather than the people called out from the world, the *ecclesia* called out from the *polis*. The effort is not to make one church united throughout the world but to make one nation under God. The church becomes simply a means to this greater end. In chapter one, the church is a means to the end of a social order dominated by elites who regard themselves as natural leaders. In chapter two, the church is a means to an end of broadening access to the advantages enjoyed by the hitherto self-styled natural leaders, a process known as justice. In both cases, the church serves the greater end of underwriting America's natural leadership in the world.

The second symptom is that Jesus is invisible. This could be for a number of reasons. It could be that Jesus is seen as an essentially private savior, having little to offer the public sphere of government or liberation. It could be that the social context of Jesus' ministry is unfamiliar to America since his context was that of a people under military occupation, in no position to impose norms or shape a whole society, and thus preexilic Israel, rather than Jesus, seems the more transferable social context. It could be that in a society gathered around a broad theistic understanding, the specific mention of Jesus is a step across a line, jeopardizing a Jeffersonian Unitarian consensus and opening up doctrinal conflict and sectarian identity. All these are plausible explanations, but I suggest the real reason is that all God's promises to Israel *are* being fulfilled—only not in Jesus. A nation has been called out from among the nations to be a people for God's own possession, and in its sacrifice and resurrection it takes upon itself and transforms all the pain and hope of the world. All God's promises to Israel are being fulfilled—in America. Jesus, the human Jesus rather than the personal savior, is often invisible in America because America has become Jesus. There is thus no need for the church as an end in itself because America is both the savior and the movement made possible by the savior's coming. America truly is the agent of its own and others' salvation. It has not just become the new Israel, it has become what the New Testament describes as the new Israel—Jesus. In the Gospels, it is hard to speak of the church in the presence of Jesus, and thus Pentecost seems a fitting beginning for the church. In just the same way, it is hard to speak of church in America because America is Jesus. America has assigned to itself the kingly role found in Israel and inherited by Jesus—the embodiment of the way God overcomes evil and brings life. This is the theological legacy of chapter one, a legacy that chapter two does not seriously question.[9]

Chapter Two as Pentecost

The American Revolution of 1776 was a revolution for American Christianity just as much as it was for American government. It is the key event in shaping what might be called the imagination of chapter two. A historian of the so-called Second Great Awakening, the religious revival that followed around the beginning of the nineteenth century, helpfully summarizes the significance of the revolution of 1776 in these terms:

> The Revolution dramatically expanded the circle of people who considered themselves capable of thinking for themselves about issues of freedom, equality, sovereignty, and representation. Respect for authority, tradition, station and education eroded. Ordinary people moved toward these new horizons aided by a powerful new vocabulary, a rhetoric of liberty that would not have occurred to them were it not for the Revolution. In time, the issue of the well-being of ordinary people became central to the definition of being American, public opinion came to assume normative significance, and leaders could not survive who would not, to use Patrick Henry's phrase, "bow down with utmost deference to the majesty of the people." The correct solution to any important problem, political, legal, or religious, would appear to be the people's choice.[10]

The two cultures, revival and revolution, coalesced to produce a remarkable outpouring of energy and creativity. Revival provided the drive, and revolution provided the vocabulary. Class structure, history, and tradition were widely reviled. The word *dissent*, so significant in England, simply dropped out of the dictionary in America because there was no widely acknowledged orthodoxy in the light of which dissident groups appeared unusual. The whole idea of leadership changed. No longer were clergy a separate class of men, learned in doctrine, manners, and morals. Now what counted was fluency in the vernacular idiom, rootedness in rural reality, and affirmation that the center of religion was in the hearts of its adherents. The task of preaching was no longer the tidy enunciation of salutary and edifying wisdom; now it was the evocation of ecstasy, the entry into the world of dreams and visions, and the experience of personal revelation and profound conviction. The same historian points out the significance of democratization for denominational life:

> Christianity was effectively reshaped by common people who . . . wanted their leaders unpretentious, their doctrines self-evident and down-to-earth, their music lively and singable, and their churches in local hands. It was this upsurge of democratic hope that characterized so many religious cultures in the early republic and brought Baptists, Methodists, Disciples of Christ, and a host of other insurgent groups to the fore.[11]

The consequences for American society of this powerful cocktail of revival and revolution remain to the present day. The separation between religion and government may have found its way into the Constitution, but there is no pretending that one can keep them separate in the formation of a culture. The Pentecost of religious individualism opened the door to the marketplace of economic transformation. As Hatch points out:

> Insurgent religious leaders espoused convictions that were essentially modern and individualistic. These convictions defied elite privilege and vested interests and anticipated a millennial dawn of equality and justice. Yet, to achieve these visions of the common good, they favored means inseparable from the individual's pursuit of spiritual and temporal well-being. They assumed that the leveling of aristocracy, root and branch, would naturally draw people together in harmony and equality. In this way, religious movements eager to preserve the supernatural in everyday life had the ironic effect of accelerating the break-up of traditional society and the advent of a new order of competition, self-expression and free enterprise.[12]

I am suggesting that what was taking place in this defining period of American history was an overemphasis on Pentecost, to the neglect of other aspects of God's story. By Pentecost, I mean the sense that God has bestowed his Holy Spirit on each and every person God has made, that every single person can meet God for himself or herself, unhindered by the limitations or restrictions of class, educational background, geographical location, or flawed personal history. I mean also that God is acting in profound and sometimes dramatic ways in the lives of individual believers to such an extent that they (a) might be persuaded that God's action in their lives is the very essence of the nature of God's story and (b) may then judge the significance or authority of other time-honored and widely regarded aspects of God's story by whether such aspects correspond to the character of the God who has been personally revealed to them. In the simplest terms, the day of salvation is no longer the day Christ died or the day he rose from the grave but is now the day I was born again. The story is no longer fundamentally about God: God is now a character in a story that is fundamentally about me.

I have highlighted the period of the Second Great Awakening not just because it follows the defining event in American cultural and religious history, the revolution of 1776, but also because it is perhaps the closest approximation to the golden era to which so much religious nostalgia reverts. Despite the fact that today there are more Christians in America than ever before, in almost all brands of Christianity there is a wistful declension narrative at work, in which it is assumed with an air of lament that American Christianity has lost something that it once had. If it indeed ever had that something, perhaps the Second Great Awakening was the period when it was most evident. But I am suggesting that if there are indeed things wrong today, they were at least as wrong then.

And what was wrong became fairly quickly apparent. The period after the Second Great Awakening exposes the flaws in a Christian imagination focused largely on Pentecost. In the words of another historian, Mark Noll:

> The social promise of revivalism was that converting individuals could transform society; social reform inspired by biblical holiness would grow naturally from the actions of the converted. . . . In the 1830s, however, the dream of a moral Christian society, transformed outwardly by the voluntary efforts of the inwardly converted, began to collapse.[13]

10

We may observe three aspects of this collapse. The word *we* could be described as the most troubling word in American history. One can see the theme of Pentecost, and the agenda of chapter two, as a long struggle over who got to be considered a part of that "we." One example of this is the betrayal of the Cherokee Indians. After signing a peace treaty with the U.S. government in 1794, the Cherokee of western North Carolina and surrounding areas experienced a cultural revival and a steady acceptance of Christianity. With the discovery of gold on Cherokee land in 1828, however, the Cherokee experienced massive incursion onto their lands, and federal troops put 15,000 Cherokee in detention, prior to their virtual expulsion to land west of the Mississippi. As Noll puts it, "The United States, bearing the gifts of Christian faith and democratic politics, destroyed a tribal people working hard to accept those very gifts."[14] It turned out that the Cherokee were not part of the "we" of America, Pentecost or no Pentecost.

The greatest question of the "we" of Pentecost involves African Americans. Until the 1830s, "it seemed possible that the application of conversionist Protestant energy could bring a peaceable end to the slave system."[15] But the pro-slavery movement grew stronger from this period as the anti-slavery lobby fragmented and as Southern Protestants increasingly articulated the scriptural foundations for their practice. A Christianity that focused so strongly on Pentecost, that stressed so strongly the right of every believer to read the Bible as he or she chose and interpret it as he or she saw fit, simply had no traction for the struggle to push believers squarely toward the logic of abolitionism.

Thus the third aspect of the collapse of a moral Christian society arising from the ideal of Pentecost was the Civil War. On the one hand were those who feared the limitlessness of Pentecost—who looked to the Bible as sanction for a stability of social order under the umbrella of the American Constitution. On the other hand were those who simply regarded slavery as incompatible with the Bible. Those who had tried to keep religion out of government and thus, as they saw it, avoid the religious wars that had beset Europe, found themselves, within a century of America's founding as a nation, with a religious war. The result of the war changed the minds of no one. The ideology and hermeneutic that had justified slavery were simply adjusted to underwrite racism and segregation.

The conviction that the Bible was a book whose social model could be simply read off the page by any believer who chose to pick it up suffered a profound blow, but since Pentecost was the assumed theological model of almost everyone in the conversation, no alternative was at hand.

I conclude my survey of the logic of Pentecost with the Civil War because the Civil War seems to be the most savage indictment one can imagine of what happens when one theological theme, that of Pentecost, is elevated to the point where it obscures all others. The apparent paradox that the Civil War revealed at the time, a time to which many look back as the golden era, is not in fact a paradox at all: the obsession with the principle that God was speaking to all God's people had become an idol that obscured the rather more significant issues of what God was saying and how God's people would know it was true.

Chapter One as Ascension

I turn now to the second theme that I am identifying as having exaggerated importance in what I am calling the prologue. What I mean by *Ascension* is the tension between two realities that follow from Jesus' return to the right hand of the Father. Jesus' seat at the right hand of the Father means that he is sovereign and Lord of all, that he has led captivity captive, that he has put all enemies under his feet. This strongly suggests that society after the completion of what God has done in Jesus should be shaped in a godly manner and that it must be possible to realize the kingdom of God now that the Jesus who was crucified has been declared Lord and Christ. Yet the tension arises because the second reality is that Jesus, being fully human as well as fully divine and thus not able to be in more than one place at a time, is not here. What that second reality means for government is a perennial point of controversy for the church. What concerns me here is the way it has been a particular issue in the American church.

If the key context for the Pentecost section of my argument was the revolution of 1776, then the key context for this Ascension part of my argument is the Reformation of the sixteenth century and the religious wars of the hundred or more years that followed. America has rightly been called "an experiment in constructive

Protestantism."[16] While Lutherans formed a substantial number of those who came from Europe to America with hope, one may say that "the Protestantism which stems from Luther has continued to concentrate its energies upon maintaining the freedom of the Word and has been inclined to yield to political and economic forces in what seem to be purely temporal matters. It has confidence that if the Word is not shackled it will convert rulers and rich men and so produce a paternal, loving, reasonable rule on earth."[17]

Hence the decisive influence on the imagination of American social construction was not Luther but Calvin. Calvin "was more acutely aware than Luther had been both of the necessity of restraining evil and of the danger which lay in giving human agencies unlimited powers of restraint."[18] Restraint was a device for safeguarding the individual and society from a headlong rush to destruction. Calvin believed in constitutions that kept both church and state subject to the will of God declared in Scripture and nature and that assumed their common loyalty was to the overarching kingdom of God. Meanwhile "Calvinism insisted with the thoroughness of the Hebrew prophets that God was king over every creature. . . . Not economics, nor politics, nor church, nor the physical life could be regarded as merely temporal in significance, as not involved in corruption or beyond need of restoration to the harmony of God's kingdom."[19]

The vital ingredient to comprehending this form of Protestant social construction was the Europe the Protestants had left behind. Lutheranism spent the first half of the seventeenth century in Germany fighting for its life. Calvinism had its citadel in Geneva, but elsewhere its existence was fragile. England had had a second Reformation, but its religious future was very uncertain. Thus America became

> the land of opportunity. Here Protestantism could turn from protest and conflict to construction. It not only could but needed to do so, for while there was no royal or Roman Church here against which to raise protest, neither was there any church at all. If there was no Stuart monarchy here to interfere with loyalty to the divine sovereign and his laws, save in the distance, neither was there government of any sort. There were no settled institutions defending the special privileges of the religiously, politically, or economically powerful; but by the same token there were

no social organizations of any kind to provide for orderly procedure in the contact of men with men.[20]

New England Puritanism casts a long shadow over the colonial period of American history: "New England remained at peace, its civilization incorporated Puritan ideals in the ordering of public life, exemplary cooperation existed between magistrates and ministers . . . [and,] relative to other seventeenth-century societies, the system also enjoyed an extraordinary degree of popular support."[21] The point about the Puritan social experiment is perhaps not how much it was practiced but how much it is mourned.

The great irony of Protestant migration is that so many Protestants replicated in their new environments the degrees of social domination and uniformity from which they had fled: "As these Reformed Protestants came to America, they were seeking not a private space to be religious but a free space for their religion to transform."[22] And transform it did, as one can trace the Reformers' house style in the later shaping of American democracy, individualism, voluntarism, and capitalism.

Given all that is good about the legacy of Protestant social construction in America, why then do I gather it under the theme of Ascension and hint that it may represent such a narrowing of theological focus that one might call it an idol? Let me point out one issue of principle and another of consequence.

The issue of principle is that Jesus somewhat disappears from the process of social construction. To be sure, he is benevolently overseeing events at the right hand of the Father, applauding the institution of a social order rejoicing in his name. But the details of his earthly life, the character of his reign as disclosed in the pattern of his ministry, the logic of his incarnation, and the outpouring of his humble grace are largely invisible. He is simply an absentee landlord, and Christians in America are like the first two slaves in the talents parable, eager to show they are keeping busy until the master returns. The absence of Jesus is something Dietrich Bonhoeffer pointed out in his reflections on his visit to America, entitled "Protestantism without Reformation." Here are his words:

American theology and the American church as a whole have never been able to understand the meaning of "criticism" by the

Word of God and all that signifies. Right to the last they do not understand that God's "criticism" touches even religion, the Christianity of the churches and the sanctification of Christians, and that God has founded his church beyond religion and beyond ethics. . . . In American theology, Christianity is still essentially religion and ethics. But because of this, the person and work of Jesus Christ must, for theology, sink into the background and in the long run remain misunderstood, because it is not recognized as the sole ground of radical judgment and radical forgiveness.[23]

This is why I describe Ascension as a theme that captivates American theology. The transcendent rule of God is so significant that the immanent quality of the incarnation becomes obscured. Instead of scouring the Gospels for instances of Jesus' encounters with lepers, with fishermen, and with Pharisees, the emphasis of those who shaped the American Christian imagination has focused much more on the attempts of Samuel and Saul and David and Solomon to find the pattern of a godly society in Israel. Even in the rhetoric of the great Martin Luther King, Jr., in the civil rights struggle of the 1950s and 1960s, and even in the struggle against slavery a century earlier, it is the language of exodus and covenant, the language of Moses and Joshua, rather than the language of cross and resurrection, that seems to dominate. When King dreams, he dreams of the Promised Land, not of the new Jerusalem or the bride of Christ. The danger of losing the humanity of Christ and of finding all one's imagery in the Old Testament is that, in stressing the sovereignty of God, one loses sight of the Trinity; God becomes so high and mighty that it can become hard to think of God taking human form or having any tangible interaction with the world, and so one risks lapsing into deism.

This is the principle that is at stake. And for the consequence: out of many possibilities, I suggest simply the greatest temptation to idolatry that runs through American history from the Puritans to the present day. That temptation is to regard America as not just home for Americans, but home for God, too. The modern nation state that emerged from the seventeenth century onwards said to the church, "You look after the soul, and we'll look after the body." The state's rhetoric was that Israel had disobeyed the covenant and so God had chosen to make a new covenant with the nation state instead. As a political platform, you have to say this is a winner. You just borrow everything God promised to Israel and start promising it to yourself. Britain was one of the first states to start doing this. France was not far behind, and this habit justified these two nations' colonial ambitions. It dominated Germany's self-understanding in the years leading up to and during the Second World War. It later became central to what it meant to be an Afrikaner.

Today there is only one nation left that continues this habit of regarding itself as having inherited the promises God made for Israel. There's only one nation left that has looked at the way God chose Israel out of all the peoples of the earth for reasons that will always be a mystery of grace and turned that choice into the choice of itself for the plain and simple reasons of its superior government, geography, and general beneficence. There's only one nation left that has translated God's election of Israel into the nation's election of itself. And that nation is the United States of America. Other nations have laid claim to being the new chosen people. But the United States has declared itself a "chosen people with tenure."[24] In 1992, Bill Clinton accepted the Democratic nomination to the presidency by saying that he was bringing a "new covenant." Three years later in his State of the Union address, Clinton again referred to the new covenant and recalled what he called the "first and most sacred covenant: life, liberty, and the pursuit of happiness." It is not just that the American church has appropriated all the promises God made to Israel, dubious as this appropriation may be; it is that the American nation has appropriated all these promises to itself and has retold the "most sacred" story (note those words "most sacred") not as a story in which God chose Israel but as a story in which America chose itself.

I conclude my survey of the logic of Ascension here because it seems that once Jesus is far away in heaven and his rule is perceived to be of a general but not specific nature, the center of theology is up for grabs. And it is no serious surprise that what then grabs the center of theology is America itself. For Christians in America, the subject of Christian ethics has seldom been Jesus Christ. It has invariably been America.[25] This is the peculiar idolatry of the American Christian imagination.

Speaking of Chapter Three

When I came to Duke University as Dean of the Chapel in the summer of 2005, I suggested that the role of the Chapel was to keep the heart of the university listening to the heart of God. I chose my words carefully.

Duke Chapel is a massive and awesome building occupying a very prominent location on the West Campus of the university. Close by, there is a bronze plaque quoting the purposes of the great benefactor James B. Duke, which begins, "The aims of Duke University are to assert a faith in the eternal union of knowledge and religion set forth in the teachings and character of Jesus Christ, the Son of God."[26] For some, the imposing architecture guarantees what the founding indenture proclaimed: the heart of the university is in historic Christianity, more or less culturally conditioned by America, the South, bourgeois Protestantism, or some such qualifier. These are the inhabitants of chapter one.

For others, the architecture and the indenture epitomize the skin they believe the contemporary university must shuffle off. These outward "guarantees" symbolize the cultural domination of America's key institutions by privileged white heterosexual males for whom a culturally customized Protestant Christianity was (or is) a convenient constitution underwriting their monopoly of power. From this perspective, the central agenda is a more or less combative struggle to release the suppressed cultures, beliefs, and lifestyles and to hear the voices that for so long have constituted the underside of American culture. This is the agenda of chapter two. *Diversity* is the umbrella term for these challenges to historic strangleholds. A cynic might say that diversity names the gesture the administrators of chapter three make to demonstrate that they are in continuity with chapter two and that chapter one is gone for good. But the term *diversity* obscures as much as it names. For example, the story of the American South is one that makes the historic injustice and the present imbalance of the black-white social relationship a matter of constant scrutiny and anxiety in public life. But the language of diversity often simply dissolves this highly significant relationship into a broad affirmation of gender, race, and class difference.

What I am seeking to offer here is a guide to negotiating the realities and the opportunities of chapter three. The first move, for

Christians, is to give up the aspiration or the demand to be regarded as the heart of the university. When I came to Duke Chapel it was describing itself as "the heart of a great university." As I hope is by now clear, that kind of language sounds to me suspiciously like an assertion of the culture of chapter one. By saying the role of Duke Chapel is to keep the heart of the university listening to the heart of God, I made no claim that the Chapel was the heart of the university, but I did assert that the university does have a heart. This is a way of preserving in chapter three the search for truth while sloughing off the cultural imperialism associated with chapter one.

The hermeneutics of suspicion that deconstructs all such terms as "the heart of the university" as bids for power can have corrosive side effects. It can assume that the university does not have a heart, that an institution like Duke is just a transit camp that young people pass through as they journey from Yankee bravado to Southern civility (or vice versa). It is not far from the cynicism that suggests the university is just a soulless shopping mall, a space that simply facilitates the acquiring of qualifications and the development of specialized knowledge. In some cases, this de-centered ideology is reflected architecturally by a de-centered campus—with no outstanding gathering points and no building large enough to host a substantial constituency of university members. This is a nightmare version of chapter three, in which chapter two has thrown out the bathwater of chapter one—the restricted access, the cultural imperialism, the domination by a limited race and sex and class—but has also thrown out the baby of chapter one, the aspiration to make the university a moral project. Shorn of the purpose of chapter one and the passion of chapter two, the university in chapter three can seem like a vacuum, a vacuum that words like *excellence* and *diversity* cannot fill.

Yet by framing the idea that the university has a heart within an appeal to listen to the heart of God, I was making an unambiguous acknowledgement that to speak of the heart of the university is a faith statement. It is not an architectural observation or a sociological conclusion: it is a statement of faith—that there is such a thing as the heart of a university and that it is a vision worth striving for. By speaking of the "heart of God," therefore, I was not introducing a jarring transcendent vocabulary into a previously civil and rational conversation. I was recognizing that any conversation about purpose and passion is bound to make appeals to aspirations and notions beyond the merely cognitive and that once that appeal has been acknowledged, language about God is no more strange than language about other sources of loyalty and desire, such as *freedom* or *the nation*. But the phrase "the heart of God" is carefully chosen. It is designed to be broadly recognizable to many, perhaps most, people of faith while at the same time having a specific resonance for Christians. It is a description of Christ without an assumption of shared Christian conviction. It is thus designed to articulate the way Christians in chapter three may seek to practice intellectual generosity without sacrificing creedal integrity.

I hope it is beginning to emerge how it may be possible to imagine a Christian being a public speaker at a university without such a person simply appearing to be a throwback to another era, an embodiment of nostalgia for chapter one. The first step is to recognize that in chapter three there is a widely recognized need to restore both the purpose of chapter one and the passion of chapter two—a passion and a purpose that are both needed to identify in what sense the university is a moral project. This is what I am seeking to do in using a phrase such as "the heart of the university." The second step is to demonstrate that, once one has begun to use the suprarational and even transcendent vocabulary necessary (or at least widespread) in identifying and articulating the true worth of the university, it is a short step, rather than a grand leap, to engaging the language of God. The third step is the tone of voice in which this is done, and this is why in my mission statement I used the word *listening*.

By saying the role of the Chapel is to keep the heart of the university *listening* to the heart of God, I was of course implying that the Chapel would *itself* be engaged in listening to God. The best way to encourage others to listen is by example, but I was not taking for granted that if the heart of the university listened to the heart of God then the heart of God would say exactly the same thing to the heart of the university as it said to the Chapel. Listening means hearing what is there, not hearing what one wants to hear. This begins to show the promise of chapter three, for listening is not a mode of being particularly associated with either chapter one or chapter two.

This third step in what might be described as creating an appropriate Christianity for a university in chapter three is to move from telling the institution and its members what to think and do, to encouraging them to listen. It is a further demonstration of how the renunciation of control is in fact a deeper statement of faith than the retention of control, for in chapter three, the Chapel assumes the heart of God will speak to the heart of the university, even if not in the way the Chapel might expect or even desire. Yet if the Chapel is to bring the heart of the university to a point of genuine listening, as I made clear in my installation sermon, it will not be by bullying, conditioning, or even coercing, but by cajoling and surprising, by making beautiful gestures and being disarmingly honest, by being persistent and being gentle, by being bewilderingly generous and uncomfortably truthful, by asking awkward questions and by being an example. This is the way truth is communicated in chapter three.

Conversation

The word *heart* has three connotations, all of which are significant to living in a university that recognizes itself in chapter three. *Heart* means "center." *Heart* assumes passion, sympathy, care, sensitivity, and a little impulsiveness. *Heart* directs this center and this sense of compassion toward one key virtue: love.

This brings us to the crux of the issue. Do the many passions at play in a college environment have a common core, and, if so, what might it mean to call that core "love"? If the university really does have a heart, in what does that heart consist? By speaking of the heart of the university, I was assuming that the university is a moral project, and the nature of that project I take to be a conversation. I want now to outline what it means to describe the heart of a university as a conversation.[27] I do so because I see conversation as a key characteristic of chapter three. Conversation was important in chapter one, but significant conversation partners were excluded from the discourse, thus impoverishing the conversation. Conversation is not generally associated with chapter two, which is more identified with protest and petition and demand and argument. But I believe conversation should be near the heart of chapter three.

The life of a university is a conversation in which a community and its members grow in wisdom and understanding through disciplines of study and interaction. This conversation extends to every aspect of campus life and is the underlying narrative running through every academic and social encounter. While it is focused on the classroom, it is also extended to artistic, athletic, and other creative and collaborative disciplines and to every academic, recreational, apparently casual, or incidental interaction on or in any way related to the campus. The conversation requires participants to develop and apply disciplines and skills of listening, reading, evaluating, and speaking so as to engage in dialogue with appropriate attention and appetite.

It demands that the participants listen to words that have been spoken and written over many centuries and in many cultures, words regarded then or now as good or true or beautiful, and that the participants join in a common search for truth. It assumes that they pursue the preparation of assignments or the publication of research as equipping them to join the conversation rather than purely as a means to personal enhancement. It expects that they foster connections between scholarly and experiential spheres of engagement and that they link reasoning, discernment, and empathy. It looks to them to uphold and reflect upon the principles of honesty, openness, fairness, and accountability and to aspire to enrich themselves and the human and global community through discovery and understanding, the formation of character, and the negotiation of significant disagreements.

Participants in this conversation understand that few significant aspects of their lives will be unaffected by the profound nature and demands of the conversation. They accept that they will be made uncomfortable by the relentless questioning of assumptions and the difficulty of coming to a fixed position, while also experiencing what it means to make meaningful commitments to people, places, and principles. They realize that genuine respect requires learning enough of one another's traditions and disciplines so as to make evaluative judgments about what is worth affirming. They know that they must conduct the conversation in a spirit of courtesy and civility, even in the face of significant disagreement, and they seek to hold one another accountable for behavior that inhibits, discredits, or undermines the character and commitments of a community engaged in such a conversation.

Those who join this conversation recognize that participation is a profound privilege and that no social group may be a priori excluded. They make every effort to ensure that the conversation aspires to be the best in the land, in terms of the potential and the accomplishments of the participants; their diversity of identity, experience, and thought; and the nature, quality, and fruitfulness of their engagement with one another. Finally, they offer due respect and appropriate access to staff, alumni, local residents, donors, and others who make the conversation possible.

I have taken the trouble to describe the nature of this conversation in some detail because such an exercise is so seldom done and because I take this conversation to be the heart of the university. If one can say that one loves the modern university, this conversation would, I suggest, be a worthy object of love. The conversation is that rare thing in the contemporary world—a practice that is of value for its own sake. The heart of a university lies in a conversation that relishes diversity because keeping the company of people with identities and commitments and assumptions that differ from one's own requires all members of the university to learn how to disagree—and in the process refine their own arguments, deepen their knowledge of their own and others' traditions and convictions, and occasionally—just occasionally—in the seclusion of a library or laboratory, after a seminar or a face-off, change their minds.[28]

The Christian speaker at a university that recognizes itself as being in chapter three must therefore prove himself or herself to be a worthy participant in such a conversation. Chapter three does not make such a conversation impossible; indeed, it makes the conversation more possible than ever before because some of the voices that are represented were previously excluded. That is what it means to speak of diversity as indispensable to excellence. But chapter three does make such a conversation even more necessary than ever before. Released from the burden of chairing the conversation and prevented by diversity from dominating the conversation, the Christian speaker stands to find a new voice that offers a blessing to both the university and the church, for many delight to speak of how the role Christianity took, in eras I have called the prologue and chapter one, has imprisoned the university, but few recognize how such a role has impoverished the church.

Spirit

G. W. F. Hegel speaks about three perspectives from which a person may regard a story.[29] The *epic* perspective is that of what we might call the news reporter: this person has not witnessed the events but has conscientiously brought together all the necessary materials and has ensured that his or her own assumptions and social context should not unduly color the narrative. The story becomes a kind of "given," delivered in a lapidary style that does not allow for interruption or questioning or dissent. The epic perspective is about detached, objective maturity but also about plausibility, comprehensiveness, and coherence.

The *lyric* perspective assumes that if the narrative is truly profound it will inevitably have a deep impact on the storyteller. Those who are close enough to see significant moments in an unfolding story will doubtless have a major personal investment in the way the story ends or will at least sense that the narrative has far-reaching resonances with dimensions of their own character and experience. The fact that the storyteller is so close to or almost becomes part of the story makes the narrative all the more fascinating as the listener disentangles the subjective from the more objective aspects of the account.

The *dramatic* perspective strives to synthesize the strengths of the epic and lyric dimensions. Like the lyric, it does justice to the role of the subject—the way events arise from the hearts and minds and actions of people, rather than from impersonal external forces. Like the epic, it perceives an object that has reason and validity beyond the subjectivity of the involved observer.

In the casual vocabulary of the university campus, one could reasonably accurately regard the epic account of the nature and destiny of the world as a description of "religion," and the lyric account as a description of "spirituality." Religion names the aspects of faith that are not "cool." They happen at set times. They have at least a dimension of formality about them—regularized clothes, an established sequence of actions, a pattern or ritual of movements, verbal exchanges, and prearranged music—all of which convey the hovering presence of a grand metanarrative that sets humanity in a fixed and time-honored relationship to deity and nature. Since these aspects are historic traditions, they bring with them a large amount of baggage—of truth-claims amended, of shameful exemplars refusing to remain buried, of cultural manifestations inhibiting cherished freedoms—a litany of vested interests, hushed dissent, and furtive abuse.[30]

Spirituality, faith in the lyric mode, by contrast, is "cool." It is contemporary and elastic, driven by the winds of shifting cultural norms. Lyric spirituality finds its genesis in the depths of personal experience and emotion, which are often the places where college students connect deeply with themselves and with others and where they interpret the changing world around them. Its moorings are not in the habits and rituals of religious traditions and faith communities but in the inclinations of the individual and in that which is beautiful and meaningful for the present. Lyric spirituality sometimes tends toward spirituality as commodity, and it flourishes on college campuses where students full of passion and idealism who are seeking substance and purpose find themselves swimming in a cocktail of ideas, experiences, relationships, and emotions.

A student came to see a colleague of mine at the end of his junior year at Duke. He had been rather active at Duke Chapel during his first semester on campus and then dropped out of sight for two years. He was a Protestant by birth, though his mother raised him in an Orthodox church in Romania before they came to the United States while he was in middle school. After they exchanged friendly greetings and swapped a couple of stories from the previous two years, my colleague judged it the right moment to tell him how he had missed him at the Chapel and to wonder if he might want to come back. "All my life I was taught that Christianity would make me spiritual," the student said. "I never felt spiritual in church. Actually, I've discovered that I feel more spiritual by having a smoke, playing guitar, and talking about the deep questions of life with my buddies late into the night. I've found Saint Mattress in my room to be a much more comfortable place to worship than Duke Chapel on Sunday mornings."

This description of spirituality is typical of the lyric mode. The student understands spirituality to be fundamentally feeling-oriented and centered in personal experience. The late night connection with friends around music and deep conversation is intimate and beautiful, and it gives a sense of satisfaction and joy. Lyric spirituality forgoes the traction of spirituality shaped by rituals and practices of religious communities. Its politics are profoundly conservative, and its social awareness is incidental. While it certainly provides a sense of meaning and contentment, lyric faith is enticingly relative, bending to personal feelings and desires. It lacks the depth of spiritual wisdom that religious traditions have mined and handed down over centuries.

It is not hard to see a broad correlation that identifies "religion" as an epic manifestation of what I have called chapter one and "spirituality" as an internalized lyric manifestation of what I have called chapter two. As an institutionally appointed representative of a particular faith, I often find others assume I will speak up and stand for "religion." The assumed dynamic is that I will use ancient authorities and a modest form of institutional bullying to encourage or coerce conformity to an anachronistic narrative and an outdated ethic. This is what chapter one is assumed to mean in today's language. The alternative is to celebrate the lyric and simply hold up stories of inspiring individuals and celebrate the freedoms acquired in chapter two. That aside, in public, it might seem there is nothing to say.

It might seem there is nothing to say, unless there is indeed a "dramatic" voice in which to speak. To portray faith in the dramatic mode is not necessarily to ridicule much maligned religion or much vaunted spirituality. It is to perceive the philosophical assumptions behind each and to seek to harmonize them. Behind epic "religion" is what theologians sometimes call dualism—that is, a sense that there is a "heaven" that is very separate from earth, so separate, in fact, that there is little or no point of contact. God, or some similar primal force, is fundamentally far away, at best an absentee landlord. We are left to carry out obscure instructions with little tangible reward other than the assuaging of guilt or the sense of peace that arises from establishing habit and rhythm. Behind lyric "spirituality" is a sense of the essence deep down in things, an awareness of the wonder of life and the fragility of beauty. Theologians sometimes call this paganism because it is close to the worship of each living thing and is, in many cases, in a drive to be "authentic," the worship of an abstraction called the "self."[31]

A truly *dramatic* faith announces how heaven comes to earth, that is, how the rhythms of the biological world and the psychological self are dimensions and (sometimes poor) reflections of an even deeper reality. A dramatic account infuses the language of distant absolutes with intimate longings but rises above the sentimentality of personal emotion to articulate visceral desire. Dramatic speech does not have to choose between ancient text and contemporary feeling, established ritual and spontaneous expression, time-honored truth and postcolonial critique. Instead, it seeks to articulate where the conversations between and among these discourses point sharply today.

I am suggesting that dramatic speech is the appropriate mode for chapter three. Once again, the Christian speaker discovers that chapter three, far from making Christian speech difficult, is on the contrary a gift that refines Christian speech and offers to strip away the distortions of epic religion on the one hand and lyric spirituality on the other.

Character

If there is one thing the "platform party" at a major university event is expected to dwell upon, it is character. Those who deeply mourn chapter one tend to regard character as one of the chief dimensions of college culture that has been irretrievably lost as the narrative has moved on. There is a largely unspoken assumption that at an unspecified time in the past—when the university had a heart and its members had religion—the students had character. What one supposes that character amounted to depends on one's notion of ethics.

If one assumes ethics is a matter of rule-making and rule-keeping, then character is about keeping the rules even when no one is looking. With good reason, faculty and administrators are alarmed at the spiraling increase in undeniable plagiarism. Hence Duke's Undergraduate Convocation includes an opportunity to sign an honor code and to hear a speech from an undergraduate commending the notion. From the classroom to the laboratory to the athletic field, there are countless examples and stories of why keeping the rules is a good idea.

If one's understanding of ethics is more about things that cannot be measured but can nonetheless be felt, like trust, love, integrity, authenticity, and loyalty, one is more likely to search for inspiration away from the formal setting and in sports teams, project groups, intimate relationships, and friendship circles. We often hear graduating seniors say the thing they valued most about Duke is their friendships, and many a parent knows that the biggest (and least parentally malleable) influence on a son's or daughter's character is the friendships made in college. This may be a very different understanding of character from the rule-bound notion; after all, a stern test of loyalty comes when one is asked to break a rule for the sake of one's team or friend.

There is little joy for a public speaker at university events in encouraging (or demanding) the keeping of rules. One is more likely to gain the audience's attention and interest by finding a poetic or uplifting language in which to extol loyalty, the endurance of friendships over time, or the support, challenge, and fun of a team working together through good times and bad. An almost universal expectation of a public university pronouncement is that the pronouncement will call on the audience to employ its talents in a way that benefits the underprivileged at home or abroad. (This section is in the unwritten contract with the commencement speaker.) But given the crisis of authority in regard to rule-keeping and the discomfort in relation to "religion," this appeal is almost never based on heeding a command ("just as you did it to one of the least of these who are members of my family, you did it to me," Matthew 25:40). Instead, community engagement is invariably grounded in an expanded sense of interpersonal ethics—that is, "these people, with AIDS or with low literacy skills, they are on your team too."

But what seems very difficult to speak about, in a culture that suspects that any mention of truth is a covert bid for power or a warning of subtle coercion, is what all this academic endeavor and personal striving might be for. The relentless concern with social location and identity misses the most interesting thing about members of a university: what matters most is not where they are coming from but where they are going. The future is always bigger than the past. The medieval notion of virtue is based on the idea of the quest.[32] The quest is a long journey toward a distant but specific goal, and a great deal is discovered on the way, about oneself, one's fellow travelers, and the goal itself. The virtues name those qualities one needs to develop in order to survive and thrive on the journey.[33] It really is no use beginning a public conversation about virtue and character if one is not able to join a public conversation about where an institution and the individual members of it are heading.

Reflection on the so-called religious wars of the sixteenth and seventeenth centuries discredited the notion that a conversation about teleology—about where we are all going—can be had in public without leading to mass slaughter.[34] It is widely supposed today that the only goods one can discuss publicly are instrumental goods (that is, qualifications that will take you to the next good place), not final goods (that is, ultimate goals). Again this makes speaking on significant public occasions very difficult. There is little to hope for but peace and security, a safe world in which to . . . nobody says quite what. A culture that cannot ask why is a culture doomed to lethargy and cynicism. Somebody must be permitted to speak about final goals and ultimate goods, but it is essential that that somebody is able to detach those aspirations from a cloaked coercion that forces the unwilling to head there, whether they think it looks like salvation or not.

Speaking and Preaching in Chapter Three

The sermons and addresses that are included in this volume are my best effort to describe how to speak of and live Christianity in what I am calling chapter three. In that sense, they are in continuity with the ethos and character and practice of chapter three that I describe in more systematic detail in my books *Improvisation* and *God's Companions*.

There is of course a significant difference between speaking and preaching. Most of the material in this book consists of sermons. A sermon is a liturgical event, which finds its meaning in the context of music and scripture and sacrament, of confession and creed and thanksgiving. A preacher at Duke Chapel can more or less take for granted some understanding of the authority of scripture, a good deal of respect and indeed hunger for theological reflection, and a level of shared experience of the pressing events of the day as seen from a campus perspective. If a preacher proves trustworthy in these three areas, he or she may well be invited to speak on occasions of public significance in the life of the university.

Being a speaker is different from being a preacher. It was not always so. In the period I have called the prologue, the two were at times indistinguishable. Today, however, the level of shared experience is comparable, but the respect for scripture and theology is not. I have portrayed some of the assumptions that may lie in the minds of those offering the invitation and those making up the audience. The task is not only vitally necessary but also possible, as long as one makes one assumption and takes four philosophical and rhetorical steps.

Speaking in Chapter Three

The assumption the preacher-turned-speaker must make is that most people listening will have some sense that they are living in chapter three of a story in which the previous two chapters could be called "white male cultural domination underwritten by a Protestant ideology" and "rebellion of the excluded." In this context, every Christian speaker, particularly white males, must accept that the audience will assume the message will (rightly or wrongly) be characterized by some form of nostalgia for chapter one.

The first step is that the speaker should recognize the role of the university as a *moral project*, an organism with a heart. The speaker does not represent that heart but urges all listeners to renew their stake and participation in that heart that can only be corporately discerned and renewed. The kinds of claims necessary to speak of such a corporate project are very close to the kinds of claims necessary to speak about God.

The second step is to identify that the heart of the university lies in a conversation. What is considered good in a university is what makes that conversation possible and enriches it. What is considered bad at a university is what impairs that conversation or makes it impossible. The speaker must show that he or she is making the conversation better than it would otherwise be; this is his or her only authority for speaking. The speaker must explicitly communicate that his or her remarks are not a closed-off dogmatism but an invitation to *continue a conversation* that is assumed to be in full flow before the speaker stands up to begin. This is not the last word. This is not a word that will be enforced by coercion, whether subtle or unsubtle. It is an invitation and a contribution to a conversation.

The third step is to adopt what Hegel called the *dramatic* mode. This means that the speaker must seek to synthesize the heritage of distant absolutes and the pressing demands of personal emotional fulfillment. He or she must avoid the airiness of pious platitudes as much as the sentimentality of heart-tugging anecdote. He or she should portray personal stories as aspects or illustrations of far-reaching dynamics or struggles and should ground larger claims and exhortations in the lived realities of communities and networks. His or her speech should be the place where the epic and lyric modes meet in an inspiring and searching way.

Finally, the fourth step is to pursue a *teleological* agenda. That is, the speaker should have the courage to name and display the goal to which he or she assumes the audience is or should be striving. It is not especially helpful to take time asking the audience to understand where the speaker is coming from. It is much more constructive and intriguing to say to the audience, "Would you like to go where I'm going?" If one is going to tell inspiring stories of individual or corporate virtue then it should be because those virtues have been discovered to be essential to the journey one is urging one's audience to join.

If the speaker misses the central assumption about living in chapter three, he or she will likely lose the audience altogether. If the speaker gets the first step right, concerning the moral project, he or she will gain the trust of those who mourn chapter one and the respect of those who cling to the victories of chapter two. If the speaker gets the second step right, concerning the conversation, he or she will be admired for having a generous spirit and respecting and being open to learn from those who come from different beginnings and seek different ends. He or she will, in short, be an appropriate member of a university. If the speaker gets the third step right and finds a dramatic mode, his or her address will have an electric quality that stirs the heart of its audience through humor, tenderness, direct speech, and fearless honesty, and he or she will gain a reputation for putting a finger on the mood of a whole community. If the speaker gets the fourth step right, the teleological one, he or she will be commended for attaining a note of genuine authority—settling not for the piecemeal fruits of spirituality but articulating the thrilling words of truth. In the process, the speaker will not only have found a way in which Christianity can refine the university but also a way in which the university can refine Christianity.

Preaching in Chapter Three

It may be helpful to identify how the sermons and addresses that follow exemplify the arguments made in this introduction.

The first sermon in chapter 2, entitled "Sharing God," offers the methodological key to the book. It outlines for the sake of the congregation the broad terms of the discussion engaged in this introduction. It is a plea for a practice of faith appropriate to chapter three. The conversational mode, which I describe above as so important to the tone of voice in which a preacher engages with the culture in general and the university in particular, is displayed in several sermons. For example, "The Grace Economy" in chapter 7 seeks to explore a troubling cultural theme without claiming Christianity has all the answers to it.

Moving to Hegel's dramatic mode, the sermons try to retain both personal passion and critical distance. For example in chapter 1, the sermon entitled "The Action of God and Catastrophe" explores Hurricane Katrina from several perspectives, including (but by no means limited to) the listeners' own. Likewise, "The Action of God and War" invites both epic and lyric responses while seeking to reach a dramatic synthesis. Most obviously, in the sermon "Adultery," I am working hard not to allow the congregation to regard the adulterer as someone "other" than themselves, without simply lapsing into anecdote or lyric accounts of passion, pain, or foolishness. The dramatic mode should ensure against the possible self-righteousness of the epic or the possible self-indulgence of the lyric. Similarly, the shifting perspectives of sermons such as "Identifying Discipleship" or "Homosexuality" tease the listener into assuming one of the options is preferable to the others before showing that all are necessary and vital. There is still a place for the lyric mode, particularly in times of challenge or lament, and the two orientation sermons, "The Heart of God" and "The Absence of God," seek to capture the mood of significant transitions.

Finally there is the teleological agenda of identifying what all the activity and intensity of the university is *for*. This appears in many places since it is such a central question for both preacher and speaker. Notably it is the theme of "The Divine Economy" in chapter 7 and is the assumed context for the sermons on heaven and hell in chapter 6. And it provides the force behind the climax to "In Four Words" in chapter 5.

Duke Chapel is a perfect environment in which to explore the contours of the period I have called chapter three. It is a place where preaching is treasured, in a university in which speaking is valued. This book is an attempt to continue a conversation, in a dramatic mode, of a teleological agenda. That agenda is intended to keep the heart of the university, and thus the heart of our culture, listening to the heart of God.

Notes

The Introduction draws on portions of "Say Something Spiritual: Speaking the Truth in a Culture Committed to Diversity" (with Craig Kocher), *Journal of College and Character* 7 no. 8 (October 2006): 1–7.

1. Colleges that emerge from this era and still survive include Harvard (Congregationalist, 1636), William and Mary (Anglican, 1693), Yale (Congregationalist, 1701), Princeton (Presbyterian, 1746), Dartmouth (Congregationalist, 1769), and Rutgers (Dutch Reformed, 1766). Roman Catholic colleges began to emerge with Georgetown (1789), and eight more had been founded by 1885. See the discussion opened up in Gavin D'Costa, *Theology in the Public Square: Church, Academy and Nation* (Oxford and New Malden: Blackwell, 2005), 38–56.

2. See James Tunstead Burtchaell, *The Dying of the Light: The Disengagement of Colleges and Universities from Their Christian Churches* (Grand Rapids: Eerdmans, 1998). D'Costa summarizes, for example, Burtchaell's account of the reasons for institutional change in Catholic colleges and universities in this era:

> a decline of religious orders in the 1960s, so that personnel were not available to staff universities; an increasingly secular society, leading to the decline of Catholic students and their loyalties to Catholic institutions; financial crises in these institutions requiring them both to change the curriculum to recruit students and also change their forms of governance quickly to ensure massive state aid when the question of their religious nature was questioned as being in conflict with the First Amendment (an issue only resolved in the mid-1970s, after most institutions had already changed); the low level of excellence achieved, leading to emulation of secular (latterly Protestant) rivals; a movement in the curriculum away from rigorous confessional theology to academic historically oriented study of Christianity, followed by the growth of religious studies (known by various names); the decline of worship and Catholic praxis being central to all staff and students; the decline in religious having key positions as presidents; and finally, the acceptance of modernity within lay and ecclesial circles. (D'Costa, *Theology in the Public Square*, 48)

Burtchaell also speaks of the importance of a single president in running a large institution (and therefore the opportunity for rapid change) and the increase in specialisms and the emergence of the career academic, meaning that faculty were increasingly focused on their own career prospects and research opportunities (See D'Costa, *Theology in the Public Square*, 50). Burtchaell (x) notes that (to translate his argument into my language) Catholic colleges had their chapter one during the Protestants' chapter two—in other words that the changes overcoming Catholic universities mirrored those that had taken place in Protestant colleges since the 1890s. This story is told in George Marsden, *The Soul of the American University: From Protestant Establishment to Established Nonbelief* (New York: Oxford University Press, 1994) and in Douglas Sloan, *Faith and Knowledge: Mainline Protestantism and American Higher Education* (Louisville: Westminster John Knox, 1994).

3. David Lodge, *How Far Can You Go?* (London: Penguin, 1980), 143.

4. Part of the nostalgia for chapter two in much of the "progressive" part of the American church today may be due to the sense that, in the era of marches and sit-ins, the church was closer to the prow of cultural engagement and change than at any other remembered time, before or since.

5. Oliver O'Donovan describes a very different kind of chapter two that shows how much the British context he presupposes differs from the American context I am describing. But he also seems to assume he and his readers are now in a "chapter three" climate.

> In our days it is not religious believers that suffer a crisis of confidence. Believers did suffer a serious one two or three generations ago, and the results of that crisis in small church attendance and the de-Christianizing of institutions are still working themselves out around us. But that crisis was precipitated by the presence of a rival confidence, a massive cultural certainty that united natural science, democratic politics, technology, and colonialism. Today this civilizational ice-shelf has broken up, and though some of the icebergs floating are huge—natural science and technology, especially, drift on as if nothing has happened—they are not joined together anymore, nor joined to the land. (*The Ways of Judgment: The Bampton Lectures 2003* [Grand Rapids, Mich., and Cambridge, UK: Eerdmans, 2005], xii)

Of course the British chapter one and prologue are likewise very different from the American ones.

6. "It was an evil day for Christian thought when prophecy became the fashionable category for political reflection in place of practical reasonableness" (O'Donovan, *Ways of Judgment*, xv). This seems to summarize O'Donovan's view, but in the story I have been telling, it sounds uncomfortably like the language of chapter one rather than chapter three.

7. Charles Marsh provides a very helpful and rewarding survey of the racial dimensions of what I am calling chapter two. Speaking of the Mississippi pastor and activist John Perkins, he says, "Perkins began using the term 'prophetic' to describe the counter-cultural practices of the Christian community (long before Cornel West took on the term to describe a faith imbued with the 'sobriety of tragedy, the struggle for freedom and the spirit of hope'), and he thought hard for the first time about the connection between racism in the south and national military spending, nuclear stockpiling, and the political neglect of the poor." Charles Marsh, *The Beloved Community: How Faith Shapes Social Justice, from the Civil Rights Movement to Today* (New York: Basic Books, 2005), 180. Charles Marsh has a clearer vision for the visibility of the church in chapter two than I do.

8. Frank Lambert's *The Founding Fathers and the Place of Religion in America* (Princeton, N.J., and Oxford, UK: Princeton University Press, 2003) bears out the story I have been telling. He describes the first defining moment in American religious history as 1639, when "a group of New England Puritans drafted a constitution affirming their faith in God and their intention to organize a Christian nation." He is referring to the delegates from Windsor, Hartford, and Wethersfield who drew up the Fundamental Orders of Connecticut, "which made clear that their government rested on divine authority and pursued godly purposes." The second defining moment is 1787, when the founding fathers drafted a constitution that made no reference to God or divine providence, seeking only secular, political ends. The battle since has been between those who champion a Christian nation and those who applaud religious freedom with a liberty of conscience for all (1–15).

9. It is illustrative that when an attempt *is* made to make Jesus visible, for example by John Howard Yoder, the project is widely dismissed as sectarian and assumed to be advocating social withdrawal. See J. H. Yoder, *The Politics of Jesus: Behold the Man! Our Victorious Lamb*, 2nd ed. (Grand Rapids, Mich.: Eerdmans, 1994).

10. Nathan O. Hatch, *The Democratization of American Christianity* (New Haven, Conn., and London: Yale University Press, 1989), 6.

11. Ibid., 9.

12. Ibid., 14.

13. Mark A. Noll, *The Old Religion in a New World: The History of North American Christianity* (Grand Rapids, Mich.: Eerdmans, 2002), 104.

14. Ibid., 106.

15. Ibid.

16. H. R. Niebuhr, *The Kingdom of God in America* (Chicago and New York: Willett, Clark and Company, 1937), 43.

17. Ibid., 38.

18. Ibid., 39.
19. Ibid., 39–40.
20. Ibid., 43.
21. Noll, *Old Religion in a New World*, 40.
22. Ibid., 46.
23. Dietrich Bonhoeffer, "Protestantism without Reformation," in *No Rusty Swords: Letters, Lectures and Notes from the Collected Works of Dietrich Bonhoeffer*, vol. 1, ed. Edwin H. Robertson, trans. Edwin H. Robertson and John Bowden (New York: Harper and Row, 1965), 105; quoted in Noll, *Old Religion in a New World*, 278–79.
24. Scott Bader-Saye, *Church and Israel after Christendom: The Politics of Election* (Boulder: Westview, 1999), 65–66.
25. "For [both Reinhold] Niebuhr and the social gospelers the subject of Christian ethics was America. . . . Niebuhr paid almost no attention to the social significance of the church—for finally, in spite of all the trenchant criticism he directed at America, America was his church." Stanley Hauerwas, *Against the Nations: War and Survival in a Liberal Society* (San Francisco: Harper & Row, 1985), 31, 47n22.
26. Article 1 of the Bylaws of Duke University states in its entirety that

> The aims of Duke University ("University") are to assert a faith in the eternal union of knowledge and religion set forth in the teachings and character of Jesus Christ, the Son of God; to advance learning in all lines of truth; to defend scholarship against all false notions and ideals; to develop a Christian love of freedom and truth; to promote a sincere spirit of tolerance; to discourage all partisan and sectarian strife; and to render the largest permanent service to the individual, the state, the nation, and the church. Unto these ends shall the affairs of this University always be administered. (See www.duke.edu/web/ous/bylaws00.htm)

George Marsden points out that this is the epitome of a chapter-one statement:

> The 1924 statement is a classic example of the liberal Protestant vision of a unified culture under Christ. Knowledge and religion are united in the ethics of Jesus. The implication is that all the university's goals are expressions of that unifying ethic. . . . The ideals that universities typically proclaim today are much the same as these; the only difference is that the references to the ethics of Jesus and to the church have become superfluous. Liberal Protestant theology had already located salvation primarily in social advance and so had removed any basis for maintaining a distinction between church and society. The rest of the twentieth century worked out the inevitable implication of that fusion. Public life could get on just as well, perhaps better, without the Protestant churches claiming to be at the center. (Marsden, *The Soul of the American University*, 422)

27. The following three paragraphs arose out of conversations with Noah Pickus, and the thoughts expressed are his as much as mine.

28. For the notion of learning how to disagree, see Alasdair MacIntyre, *Three Rival Versions of Moral Enquiry: Encyclopaedia, Genealogy, and Tradition* (London: Duckworth, 1990), 216–36.

29. *Hegel on the Arts: Selections from G.W.F. Hegel's Aesthetics or The Philosophy of Fine Art* abridged and translated by Henry Paolucci (New York: Frederick Ungar, 1979), 142–200. I explore Hans Urs von Balthasar's use of Hegel's categories in my *Improvisation: The Drama of Christian Ethics* (Grand Rapids: Brazos and London: SPCK, 2004), 46–53.

30. I am grateful to my colleague Craig Kocher for helping me articulate this and the following three paragraphs.

31. For a contemporary and highly accessible account of the flaws in "pagan" and "dualist" approaches, see N. T. Wright, *Simply Christian: Why Christianity Makes Sense* (San Francisco: HarperSanFrancisco, 2006).

32. See Alasdair MacIntyre, *After Virtue: A Study in Moral Theory*, 2nd ed. (London: Duckworth, 1985), 219.

33. The definitive medieval account of the virtues is that of Thomas Aquinas. He discusses the theological virtues of faith (including knowledge and understanding), hope (including fear), and charity (including love, joy, peace, mercy, beneficence, almsdeeds, and fraternal correction), and the cardinal virtues of prudence, justice (including devotion, prayer, adoration, sacrifice, vows, and oaths), fortitude (including magnanimity, patience, and perseverance) and temperance (including honesty, abstinence, and fasting). See his *Summa Theologiae* IIa IIae qq 1-148 (New York: Benziger Brothers, 1948).

34. For one of the more influential exponents of this general view see Jeffrey Stout, *Ethics after Babel: The Languages of Morals and their Discontents* (Boston: Beacon, 1988). For a contrary view, see William Cavanaugh, *Theopolitical Imagination: Discovering the Liturgy as a Political Act in an Age of Global Consumerism* (Edinburgh and New York: T & T Clark, 2002).

1

Speaking the Truth about God

The Action of God

One of the ways in which I seek to bring encouragement and indeed inspiration to a congregation in preaching is to give them a sense that there is nothing they should be afraid to consider in the light of faith. This is a university community, and one of the first issues in relation to the parting of the Red Sea (Exodus 14) is, "Did it happen?" The only way to avoid a faith/science divide is for faith to take on the big issues with an evident relish but an appropriate humility. The first half of the sermon is concerned with creating this delicate balance. I acknowledge that here we are talking about a miracle, that miracles threaten to separate faith and reason, and that responses to this tension have sometimes been unsatisfactory, even hilarious. The overall mood is designed to suggest that Christians have no need to protect God. The second half of the sermon then goes on to outline the existential and christological manner in which I suggest the story should be read. Rather than allow the matter to become an intellectual investigation or be dismissed as a metaphor or legend, I seek to take the issues more seriously than the listener might have supposed at the outset. While the theological points are significant, the principal goal of the sermon is to communicate confidence in God in the face of doubt.

About three years ago, I taught a class of third graders in an elementary school in a socially deprived part of England. I gathered the children in a circle and rolled out a large sandy-colored piece of burlap, saying "This is the desert." I took some little wooden figures out of a box and said these were the children. The children were so hungry that their parents took them a long way to find food. I moved the little wooden figures to the far corner of the burlap to represent the children crossing the desert and reaching

Egypt. I told how the people found food and how the children grew to be a great number of people but that these people came to be the slaves of the pharaohs who gave them food. I told how one night they escaped and rushed to the Red Sea. I unfolded a piece of deep blue burlap to represent the sea. I told how their leader Moses raised his arm and prayed to God and how God made a way for them through the sea, and I moved the wooden figures through the sea, one by one. Then I showed them how Miriam led the dancing on the dry shore. (You can do a lot with wooden figures.) Then I said, "I wonder where you are in this story." They each took one of the figures and explained where they chose to put them. Some were dancing; some were just about to cross the sea; some were halfway; some were still in slavery. But one said, "I know this isn't true because I saw it on the TV."

What might it mean to say that the story of the crossing of the Red Sea is true? That class of third graders discovered two contrasting notions of truth. Leaving aside the question of whether you can believe anything you see on the TV, especially when Disney gets its hands on it, they were discovering the way a scriptural story can come alive in your experience, when suddenly one of them introduced the question of historical fact. I want to explore with you why historical questions about this and other miracles are important but why getting stuck on such questions may restrict our openness to receive everything God has to give us in these stories.

The question "Did it happen?" quickly stops being a historical enquiry because the Old Testament is the only written source available and the archaeological evidence is thin. Instead it tends to become a scientific question. We all know that large movements of water brought about by spontaneous strong winds are unknown— at least, we thought we knew that. Hardly a year goes by without a new book suggesting there might have been a volcanic eruption in the Mediterranean in the time of Moses which may have caused the Red Sea to part, or something similar. Such accounts seem to me to miss the point of the story, which is to emphasize the miraculous hand of God.

Seeing no inherent plausibility in the Exodus account, historical critics 120 years ago asked how the account came to be written. They speculated that it was in fact a blend of three accounts, one that talked about the wind blowing the sea away all night so the land was dry, a second that talked about the spontaneous parting of two walls of water, and a third that didn't mention water at all. This view has never achieved a scholarly consensus, but it has always seemed to me to beg the question of *why* these accounts came to be written. The people who wrote these accounts saw them as the most momentous events in the history of the world. That at least means that any reader, whether believer or skeptic, should take them very seriously.

For many people, the problem with miracles like the crossing of the Red Sea is not a historical one. They assume that if God had what it took to create the world then God presumably had the ability to suspend these laws for a few minutes now and again. More significant for these people are the philosophical or moral questions miracles leave unanswered. If God intervened to save the Israelites, why didn't God intervene to save the New Orleanites? If God saved the Hebrews from Pharaoh, why didn't God save them from Hitler? If God held back the waves of the Red Sea, why didn't God hold back the planes on September 11?

I grew up in the Church of England, a church with a suitably confused response to such questions. When David Jenkins was consecrated bishop in York Minster in 1984, his appointment was highly controversial because he asked these questions in a particularly vivid way. A week later, the south transept of the Minster was destroyed in a fire. Some more conservative Christians started saying that God had struck the Minster as a sign of displeasure at the church consecrating a priest who had publicly questioned God's miracle-working activity. "Was this fire an act of God?" one of the cathedral canons was asked. "We no longer believe in an angry God who arbitrarily intervenes in such a way," he said soberly, and then added, briskly, "But I will say that it's a miracle that the rest of the building was saved." This is called having it both ways.

The moral problem with miracles is compounded on the occasions when they don't suit everybody. Pushing back the waves is quite a stunt and doesn't seem to hurt anyone, but crashing those waves back down on the pursuing Egyptians isn't much fun for the Egyptians. It seems legitimate to ask whether a God who could deliver the Israelites from slavery could not have done so in a less bloodthirsty manner. Because of such concerns some religion scholars have come to call the story of the crossing of the Red Sea a "myth"—that is, a foundational story of a people, but one that is not subject to the historical or moral strictures expected of most formative stories.

While I find these moral and historical questions interesting, I have to say they lack two elements that I'm going to suggest are the key to reading stories of this kind. Whenever we read the more historically and morally challenging parts of the Bible, I propose we keep the following two guidelines in mind.

The first is that these stories really matter. Working out where we are in them, as the third graders discovered in the classroom, isn't just an intellectual exercise. It is about the social, economic, emotional, political, and cultural hearts of our lives. This is a story about people in slavery, and it's bound to be hard to read if nothing in one's life remotely corresponds to slavery. I grew up in Bristol, England, a city that grew rich on the profits of the slave trade. So when I read this story, I have to engage with the reality that I am one of the Egyptians. Slavery doesn't just weigh heavily on America's conscience, you see. But my maternal grandparents were Jews, and they and my mother were also refugees who, like people from the Gulf Coast and like the Hebrews, ran for their lives and had to leave everything behind. So a part of me engages with the Israelites in this story, yet I have spent a while living in both Israel and the West Bank and have talked with conscientious Israeli Jews and equally conscientious Palestinian Christians. Both think this is *their* story, their story of liberation. Both think *they* are the slaves in this story, and both from time to time fall into thinking that if liberation comes then, as in this story, there are bound to be casualties.

So for lots of reasons this story *matters* to me, and when the third graders asked me where I would put *my* wooden figure—in slavery, in the sea, or on safe dry land—I was totally absorbed in this story, and the answer seemed to tell the truth about my life. That's how we should read this story, as a story that exposes the truth about our lives.

The second guideline to remember in reading the historically and morally challenging stories in the Bible is simply this: the Bible is about Jesus. It wasn't that Jesus was God's last resort when things had got to a pretty pass: Jesus was God's plan all along. And the central event that focuses all God's plans for Jesus and all God's plans for us is Jesus' resurrection. A miracle. *The* miracle. The definitive miracle by which all other miracles are to be judged and in relation to which all other miracles are to be understood. Here is the defeat of death, the exposure of the folly of sin, the dismantling of the power of evil. The reason the crossing of the Red Sea matters so much is that when the early Christians came to terms with the enormity of what had happened in Christ, they looked back to the Exodus. They saw sin and death and evil as slavery, they saw the cross as the raging waters of the Red Sea, and they saw the dry land as Jesus' resurrection. They saw the whole event as a story about Jesus. Because it was a story about Jesus, they realized it was *the kind of thing God would do.*

Quickly the early Christians set about embodying the story of the crossing of the Red Sea as the story that summarizes God's purposes for saving us. The way they did that was in baptism. They began the baptism ceremony with a recognition that our lives are in slavery and God longs to set us free. They then plunged the candidates into water, echoing the danger and the drowning of the Red Sea experience. Then they clothed the new Christians with resurrection robes, safe on dry land.

So just like the earliest Christians, when we read stories of miracles in the Bible or when we hear stories of miracles today, we ask ourselves, "Is this a story about Jesus? Is it about Jesus laying down his life and overcoming evil because he longs to set us free and restore us to friendship with him?" In other words, "Is it the kind of thing God would do?" Then we seek to order our life so as to create the kind of spaces where God does such things. Christians have long been associated with hospitals and classrooms because these are places where, over the centuries, God has countless times laid down his life and set people free. Christians have put huge efforts into worship, pastoral care, personal prayer, and small group nurture for the same reason. These are places where, over and again, God acts in ways like the way God acted in Jesus.

"Did the crossing of the Red Sea happen?" is an interesting question. "Is it fair?" is an important question. What is more significant, I suggest, is to explore where *we* are in this story and what God may be saying to us through it about slavery and power in our lives and in the world today. More significant still is to explore where *Jesus* is in this story, to realize that he faced the horror of the

41

crashing waves so that we might reach the safety of the dry land, and to explore how we can shape our lives in response to meeting Jesus in this story.

Then, and perhaps only then, we can come back to our original questions. Then, and only then, can we say, with humble yet confident gaze, "This is the kind of thing God would do. Yes. This is the kind of thing God would do."

The Action of God and Catastrophe

One thing I have learned about leadership in general and preaching in particular is that you earn people's respect and gratitude when you stand in front of them and face the facts, even if the facts are awful. Hurricane Katrina struck while my family's ship container of furniture finally arrived after its Atlantic voyage. I spent thirty-six hours pretending that my thoughtful sermon on Matthew 18 would do, but by Saturday night it was clear it would not. This was the result of a late evening's attempt to face the truth about God, so-called natural evil, and America. It is quoted back to me perhaps more than any of my sermons, for a number of reasons.

One is that, in touching on the atonement model of penal substitution, I trespassed onto a theme that I soon discovered was regarded as off-limits for many, perhaps most, mainline Christians. I simply used the full resources of the theological repertoire in a case of profound philosophical searching, in an effort to restate God's almightiness against an implied sense that something other than God brought Katrina. Another is that I referred to global warming, a move seen as "political" by some and unscientific by others. I did so because I wanted to engage the sense of anger that I regarded as legitimate, while keeping it only one part of the story.

Most of all, the sermon is quoted because when it came to the key words "Time, like an ever rolling stream,/Rolls all its sons away," and "Our shelter from the stormy blast/And our eternal home," I sang them, unaccompanied, in my very average faltering voice. That, for many people, seemed to express the fragile heart of faith on that day.

> The sermon uses a good deal of rhetorical technique in that, as it introduces each of the first two of the four themes, it suggests it is doing so only in passing. The center of the sermon truly is the reflection on the Trinitarian God and the presence of God in Katrina, despite all. In introducing that reflection by first passing through nature and America, however, I sought to acknowledge some important issues while still affirming that the key questions were about God. The ending is likewise not quite what it seems. It seems to suggest that the big issue is about us. This is an attempt to offset the sheer powerlessness involved in seeing thousands of stricken people close enough to be us but far enough away to be hard to help, but the shape of the whole sermon makes it clear that the focus of attention on this day is not really us at all.

How do we begin to make sense of the bewildering pictures and heartbreaking horrors emerging from Louisiana and Mississippi this week? I want to look with you at four ways of telling the story of Hurricane Katrina, each of which has a different central character.

The first story, and most visually absorbing, is a story about nature. Here is a massive wind and a colossal flow of water. These are forces of nature too big to fit in a television screen, too awesome to be described by even the most accurate eyewitness. Nature is not just about ripe fruits in gardens or soft refreshing rain; it is not just about purple headed mountains or rivers running by. Nature is about terrible destruction and ghastly death, about drowning and suffocation and terror and desperation. Meanwhile human nature, it seems, is about both ingenuity and cruelty, about both humbling generosity and opportunistic wickedness. This week we have seen the truth about nature, as a force in the heart of the earth and as a force in the human heart, but underlying the story about nature is a lingering suspicion. The suspicion is that the earth's climate is changing. The concern is that, unless something changes quickly, the whole world is going to see a lot more of the terrorism of nature and a lot less of the ripe fruits in the garden. The rest of the world sees America as a country whose leaders assume that this change of climate is not their problem. Climate change has hitherto seemed only to have affected far away places like Bangladesh. Well this week New Orleans turned into southern Bangladesh. This week the change in the world's climate became America's problem.

The second story, and the part of the story that has fascinated the chattering classes around the world, is a story about America. America is a country used to extremes of weather, along with extremes of much else. How many of us would be living in North Carolina if air-conditioning had never been invented? It gets pretty hot here. Everyone who lives by the coast in Louisiana, or in North Carolina for that matter, knows perfectly well that when a warning comes, they need mighty quick to secure their homes, get in their cars, and head to their other home or, in the event that they don't have a second home, for their relatives or a hotel some way inland. But what if you don't have a car, what if you don't have handy relatives, what if you don't have money for a hotel? This week we have found the answers to those questions. You die. If you don't die, you enter the nightmare of squalor known as the Superdome. The irony is almost too painful to point out: Americans are used to sitting back in the sofa and admiring the sporting skills of those who grace the Superdome, a great theatre of dreams, but this week Americans have gazed at the Superdome in horror as a theatre of nightmares. Is this the same America that conquered the moon in eight years and Iraq in three weeks? The hurricane has exposed the way America has come to tolerate grotesque extremes of wealth. Of the thirty thousand people in the Superdome, no more than one hundred were white. How many more people throughout America are living in economic and social conditions that leave them vulnerable to the terrorism of nature? And why has all of this apparently taken America, or at least its government, by surprise?

And the third story, again with its distinctive central character, is a story about God. The great hymns are deeply aware of the relationship between God and the forces of nature: "Time, like an ever rolling stream, / bears all who breathe away." Well the rolling stream has certainly borne a few good people away this week. "Our shelter from the stormy blast / and our eternal home."[1] Well there hasn't been much shelter to be had from the stormy blast this week, and rather a lot of people have been looking for an eternal home, having been swept away from their earthly one. For all our interest in the first two stories, about nature and about America, as

Christians we are bound to focus on this third story, the story about God. Where is God in Hurricane Katrina?

In a few moments we shall stand to say the words "We believe in God, the Father Almighty." If we truly believe God is almighty, well may we come to God in horror at this catastrophe in God's created order, well may we rail against God for the many injustices of the story—the loss of life, the punishment of the poor, the devastation of livelihoods. Well may we pray to God for mercy for the survivors, succor for the devastated, strength for the rescuers. Deep may we ponder the mystery of God's creative purpose, the beauty of wind and wave and yet the ghastliness of hurricane and flood. And anxiously may we fear God's anger against those who reject God's grace and mercy, those who harden their hearts against the destitute, exploit the desperate, and withhold the abundance of God's good gifts from those in plight and scarcity.

But let not that be all we say about the story of God. Let us remember, when we wonder why God doesn't do something, that God has already done something. God has given us good ways to live and has countless times sought to persuade us to follow these good ways, whether by rescue or warning or example or threat. This is what the Old Testament is all about. God has come among us, and by word and wonder and purpose and parable God has offered us the gift of life through friendship with God. This is the story of the New Testament. Of all the catastrophes of the world, one stands alone: the catastrophe that we rejected God's loving offer in Jesus. Jesus died a terrible death. However low we go, even to the Superdome itself, we need never look up to Jesus—only sideways. He went that low too. All God's anger against human depravity—and we have seen plenty of depravity this week, in many aspects of this tragedy—all God's anger was experienced by Jesus on the cross. Most important, however, death was overcome. The horror of nature, its death and destruction, does not have the final word. Easter has the final word. So let's never say, "How can God do nothing?" for God has already done everything. The one thing God hasn't done is obliterate us. He did that to Jesus instead. Can you believe it?

After the resurrection, God sent the Holy Spirit to transform and empower the people, to turn sorrow into dancing and waste places into springs of joy. We have seen the Holy Spirit this week. We have seen ordinary people offer moments of breathtaking kindness. We have seen glimpses of remarkable goodness, sacrificial selflessness, disarming generosity. There is no room on my boat: I shall swim so you can step on board. There is no more food: you can have mine. You have lost everything: everything that is mine is yours to share. You have no home: my home is your home. We have seen the Holy Spirit this week. So again, let not our ponderings about God's goodness or our anxieties about God's power blind us to the activity of the Spirit. God is anguished, but God is alive, and God is active.

The heart of Christian faith is the mystery of the Holy Trinity, and the heart of Christian faith today, in the wake of Hurricane Katrina, is to believe not just in the apparently removed creator God, not just in the deeply co-suffering Son of God, and not just in the empowering and surprising Spirit of God, but in all three. God is not a buffet meal from which we take just the bits our appetite and our waistline incline us to choose today. The heart of Christian faith is to take the Father, the Son, and the Holy Spirit together, *and believe that they are one God*, and that in creation there was already the suffering and empowering at work, and that on the cross there was the deep mystery of the Father and the profound subversion of the Spirit likewise at work. So if this week is a story about God, our response is first of all to pray and second to say humbly but thoughtfully, "We believe in one God."

And that leaves just one story. One more story about Hurricane Katrina, with its distinctive central character, and maybe the most uncomfortable story of the lot. This is a story about us. Where is nature in this story? That's a scientific question. Where is America? That is an ethical question. Where is God? That's a theological question. Where are you in this story? That's a personal question. Keep me out of this. I don't answer personal questions.

Well maybe it's time we did. Where are we in this story? Inspired by the Holy Spirit to get involved, do what we can, and somehow bring some good? Identifying with Jesus, crucified perhaps by waiting for news of family or friends? Or are we the safe, distant observer, either binging on horror or retreating into wisdom after the event? Hurricane Katrina has revealed the truth about nature: it is always a potential terrorist at our door, never to be underestimated, and capable of causing unimaginable destruction.

Hurricane Katrina has revealed the truth about America, that it is a nation that tolerates potentially catastrophic levels of poverty, has still not come to terms with the racial dimension of its social inequalities, and ignores climate change at its own as well as others' peril. Hurricane Katrina has revealed the truth about God, that however mysterious his ways God has definitively acted in a way that costs him everything and denies death the last word. But has Hurricane Katrina also revealed the truth about us? When you see those pictures, do you react as a child of nature, a fellow American, or a child of God? Nature has always been dangerous, America has always been a land of extremes, and God has always loved us. What have we always been? Perhaps the question for us is, "What have we always been like? And is it time to face the truth?"

The Action of God and Human Sin

The following two addresses were delivered out-of-doors, to around four hundred people on each occasion. The first was at a student-organized commemoration held on the fifth anniversary of the September 11 attacks. This was one of the very few times I have felt deeply conscious of not being American. Rather than apologize for this, I chose to take the conversation to a place where a university community had a direct interest: the language in which the events are now conventionally described. In some ways this is designed to be an example of what it means to think theologically in a secular environment. The vocabulary of the event is suffused with religious imagery, but there is no permission to speak from an explicitly Christian perspective. My rhetorical strategy was to build a strong sense of credibility in terms of articulating a view of the attacks which took them seriously as crimes and, having done so, to take the risk of making an explicitly theological point before closing. The perspective of the address repeatedly shifts between considering the events as insiders (an attack on America) and outsiders (an attack on Washington, D.C., and New York) and as a theologian (offering critique) and pastor (offering comfort).

The second address followed the shootings at Virginia Tech, at an event that took place only twenty-four hours after the news broke. This was designed to be an event open to people of all faiths. The address is much less analytical because the news was too raw to be considered cerebrally. The question of gun control was on many consciences, but events of this kind seem only to reinforce what people already believe rather than to change minds, so I chose to focus on the fragile beauty visible in a web of relationships, affirming the sense of involvement so widely felt on a campus only two hundred miles from the one affected.

September 11

September 11 is a day of the greatest horror most of us can imagine, but underlying that horror is a host of metaphors, associations, and narratives that are commonly used to characterize the shocking events, to make them somehow comprehensible. I want to talk briefly about three of the most commonly used words in the conversations surrounding this day, and I want to comment on each one from a theological point of view.

The first word is *sacrifice*. September 11 brings us face-to-face with two ideas of sacrifice. The first is sacrifice as a transitive verb—something one does to others. This is what a suicide bomber means by sacrifice. Obscuring from his or her imagination any personal details that would make mass murder grotesque and unimaginable, the suicide bomber coldly and deliberately sacrifices dozens or thousands of strangers in some kind of offering to a ghastly deity. It is a sacrifice that is prepared to lay down its life that others may die. The fireball, the trembling, and the overwhelming dust of Ground Zero are all part of this notion of sacrifice.

The other kind of sacrifice is an intransitive verb. It is an offering one makes, not of others, but of oneself. It is the sacrifice of the firefighter, the honest bystander, the selfless colleague. It is a sacrifice that is prepared to lay down its life that others may live. It is a gesture that takes us back to the root meaning of the word *sacrifice*—"to make holy." That most hideous day in contemporary history was in part made holy by those saints who laid down their lives that others might live.

If we wish to retain the word *sacrifice* in our language, this is what we must learn from September 11. Sacrifice is not something you can make another person do. It cannot be imposed. Sacrifice is something only you can do yourself. We have a name for those who are determined to take others with them to an early violent death. We call those people murderers. We have a name for those who are prepared to risk their own death in order to free others from an early violent death. We call them martyrs. We call them martyrs because a martyr is a witness and because holding onto a person or a principle up to one's last breath is the greatest witness a person can make. Those who offered their lives in this way held on to both a person and a principle. That's what makes them so special.

The second word is *tragedy*. We loosely use the word *tragedy* when we want to refer to a sad event but don't want to get into the details of blame or perspective. More precisely we refer to the heritage of Greek tragedy, a genre of theatre that concentrated on exposing the deep workings of fate and the folly of human presumption in supposing to stand above or beyond such workings. I don't believe it is right to call September 11 a tragedy. I do suggest there are two other words we should use instead. The first, secular, word is *crime*. September 11 was mass murder on a colossal scale. I don't think it is helpful to talk about it as an act of war. Flying planes into buildings is a crime. Calling it "evil" doesn't help. It is simply "wrong." "Evil" is simply saying "wrong" with a loud voice. It raises the rhetorical temperature, but it correspondingly makes clarity more difficult. September 11 was a crime. Those who planned it, executed it, and plan to do similar things again must be arrested, tried, and kept from doing further harm. To call this process a war simply allows the perpetrators of the crime a moral credibility they don't deserve.

The other word, besides *crime*, that we should use in place of tragedy is a theological one. It is *heresy* or, to use a more emotive word, *blasphemy*. The one who kills for the sake of faith is a blasphemer because he or she desecrates the one thing on which God has set God's image, human life itself. September 11 destroyed that which does not belong to us—the myriad detail of the lives of strangers. It claimed to do so in service of God, but a god who would delight in such service is nothing but a monster. So September 11 is not a tragedy. It is a crime and a blasphemy.

And the final word is *suffering*. It would be wrong to dwell too long today on the perpetrators and their ghastly parody of martyrdom, faith, and glory. Today is centrally about those who woke up one morning to a sky of azure blue and whose lives a short while later had been turned to dust and ashes by horror, death, or loss. And people of faith are bound to ask where God is in all this. For Christians, God is never a faraway deity twiddling his thumbs while we suffer. God is centrally revealed in a suffering man, Jesus, dying in agony. On September 11, the God of Jesus Christ is at Ground Zero. But while Jesus is the heart of God, he is not the whole of God. God the Holy Spirit was present on September 11 in those very gestures of self-sacrificial love of which we have already spoken. God the Father's heart is broken by a mixture of unending love for God's creation and hatred against the sin that defiles it, hence the Christian belief in a day of judgment when those who suffer are vindicated, when evil is buried, and when all tears are dried.

In the face of suffering, I have only one piece of pastoral advice, and it is this. If it can't be happy, make it beautiful. There are many things that can never be happy, and September 11 is one of them, but we can still make this day beautiful. That is what we are doing together at this present moment. I believe that is the best way to express our sadness and to honor the lost.

September 11 is a witness to the untold damage perverted religion can do, but the answer is not to renounce one's faith. Even those who seek secular answers find themselves using religious language much of the time. The only answer is to seek a truer faith, one that does not involve the sacrifice of others, one that does not become powerless in the face of apparent fate, and one that transcends suffering with the promise of final reconciliation and peace with God.

Virginia Tech

Yesterday confronted us with two of the most powerful human emotions: terror and love. The ghastly events at Virginia Tech hit us in the pit of our stomachs because they go to the heart of our physical, fragile, common humanity.

When you wander around a college campus, you don't just see a host of vibrant human beings; you see myriad people whose every move is the subject and the result of an immeasurable tide of love: from parents, siblings, grandparents, friends, teachers, mentors, coaches, peers, and colleagues. If we truly learned to see any single person in his or her complexity and in the glory of the way he or she is fearfully and wonderfully made, we would be overcome by awe that such a creature could biologically exist, physiologically live, and psychologically thrive. Faculty and staff are really no different from students in that way. They too are prisms that host a rainbow of the loves and hopes and dreams of others.

Yet alongside such wonder is unspeakable horror. If we choose—and modern technology has given us such choices—if we choose to flick a switch on a gadget and end any number of these beautiful, awesome lives, we can. Those simple gunshots, with no fanfare, only silence in between, confront us with the banality of terror. We can, it seems, blow away such a deftly crafted and deeply cherished life as simply as a child picking a flower. Yesterday, someone did just that. And a massive community is brought to its knees. A community had been going about its early morning business, a business that seemed normal, but we now can see how much unspoken love and wonder and fragile beauty it took for granted. A community that did not just reside in Blacksburg, Virginia, but also through a spider's web of parents, extended families, alumni, friends, and former employees, even sometime sporting rivals, stretches far and wide. Because we are people of imagination, it's a community that stretches right here, right now, because we know, instinctively, that we are not immune, that if it happened there it could happen here, and we are gripped by a fear that turns all our cherishing, all our nurturing, all our normal getting along into an anxious grasping to know that those we love are safe, that they will promise never to be exposed to danger, and always to know how much they mean to us.

A community of love knows the searing horror of sudden, violent, merciless loss. A community of imagination doesn't need too many explicit details, for it can visualize the hideous events quite easily. We've gathered today because we are speechless with horror, through terror, through imagination, through love. What confronts us is the limitless harm one person can do. One person's mindless cold-blooded anger can trample down the wonder, the joy, and the love of millions. That is the power we give one another over our lives.

For those of us who are people of faith, we are given a glimpse through these events into a reality we don't often perceive. For a moment we see the world as God sees it—full of wonder, beauty, fragile glory, and passionate devotion and yet, at the same time, cruelly mutilated by violence, horror, and terror. We see it that way today. God sees it that way every day. It breaks our hearts. It breaks God's heart. It is the cost of love.

The Action of God and Miracle

Before I preached this sermon, I asked a number of people whether they'd heard a sermon on the virgin birth before. I couldn't find anyone who said they had. Since I'd never heard one myself, I sensed there might be something interesting going on here. It seemed as though the virgin birth had become a doctrine that mainline Protestantism no longer had much use for, a doctrine associated with a bunch of issues—such as negative views of sex, perhaps of women, a tendency toward the far-fetched—with which enlightened mainliners aren't generally seen in public.

And yet it's hard to address almost any of the readings generally assigned for the Sunday before Christmas and not have this question staring you in the face. How do preachers so often manage to dodge the question? As with other sermons in this chapter, the principal aim of this sermon is to deepen the congregation's confidence in the gospel—and trust in the preacher—that there is no subject beyond the critical and faithful engagement of theological exploration. Far from being simply a litmus test of ecclesial conservatism, the virgin birth emerges as an introduction to a whole way of reading history and the Bible—exactly what the Gospel of Matthew seems to think it was. I tried to highlight this by calling the sermon "The Genesis of Jesus."

In a few moments' time, we shall stand and say the creed together. We'll say we believe Jesus was "conceived by the Holy Spirit" and "born of the virgin Mary." It may not be news to you to hear that for the last 150 years or so it's been quite fashionable to disbelieve in the virgin birth. Those who love conspiracy theories happily jump to the conclusion that Jesus' real father was a Roman soldier. Those who think Christianity is really a synonym for common sense or social justice tend to ignore the virgin birth as irrelevant. But Matthew doesn't think the virgin birth is a conspiracy or an irrelevance. Remember that even though his Gospel is amazingly short and his Greek is nothing classy, Matthew believes he is writing the most important words that have ever been written. Every event, indeed every word of his Gospel, is like the virgin Mary herself: laden with meaning, pregnant with significance.

So what is the meaning of the virgin birth? To start with, Mary is the new Eve. The Old Testament begins with Eve, a woman who causes trouble for her husband by saying yes to sin. The New Testament begins with Mary, a woman who causes trouble for her husband by saying yes to salvation. Whereas Adam is a pushover who compounds his sin by trying to cover it up, Joseph is a righteous man who realizes he can't marry Mary but shows extraordinary mercy by not making a public spectacle of her and banishing her from the garden of respectability. Mary and Joseph together get right what Eve and Adam together got wrong, so Mary is a new Eve.

And the next layer of meaning is that Mary is a new Abraham. Abraham obeyed God's call to leave his known land and go to a place that God had made ready for him. Through the obedience of the one man Abraham, all the families of the nations came to be blessed. Mary and Joseph also left their known land and went to a place that God had made ready for them. Through the obedience of the one woman Mary, all the families of the nations received a blessing. Mary is the new Abraham. Abraham is the father of Israel; Mary is the mother of the Church.

Matthew tells us the two names by which Mary's son is to be known. One name is Jesus, or literally Yeshua, which means "salvation." This tells us what the child of Mary and Joseph's obedience is to do: he is to be the new Joshua, who is to bring salvation by leading his people into a new Promised Land. The other name is Emmanuel, which literally means "the with-us God." The name Emmanuel shows us who Mary's son is—God with us. The name Yeshua tells us what Jesus does—he saves us.

But this is not all. Matthew makes explicit reference to the prophecy of Isaiah: "Hear then, O house of David! . . . The young woman is with child and shall bear a son, and shall name him Immanuel" (7:13-14). This prophecy speaks to the house of David, and Matthew takes it as a promise that Mary's son will be the son of David—like David himself, restoring Israel to its glory, or like David's son Solomon restoring the Temple, or at least restoring the intimacy between the people and God that Israel had looked to the Temple to guarantee. But the prophecy is set during the time of Ahaz, who was king of Judah around 735 B.C., and presided over a disastrous time when God's people were devastated by an Assyrian invasion. The remarkable birth prophesied in the eighth century B.C. is in a similar context to the birth of Jesus many centuries later: both are rays of hope in a time of foreign occupation when the Jewish leaders have let their people down.

So Matthew sees layer after layer of significance in a virgin conceiving a son. There's Eve, there's Abraham, there's Joshua, there's David and Solomon, there's deliverance from sin and oppression. What it all amounts to is this: the Old Testament frequently refers to Israel as a young woman. There's a general rule of thumb that whenever the Gospel writers speak about Mary, they have in the backs of their minds a notion that this young woman symbolizes Israel. So what the virgin birth means to Matthew is that Israel could not by itself bring about its own salvation. It couldn't, if you like, *conceive of* its own salvation. But God had chosen never to be except to be in relationship with us—he is, after all, the With-us God, Emmanuel. So the virgin birth shows how salvation is wholly *God's* initiative, but *Israel*, represented by Mary, is *integral* to the coming of God. Later theologians would formulate the principle that Jesus is fully human and fully divine, which simply expresses the same point in a different way. God could live, could save, on his own, but he chooses to live and save with us. That's what the virgin birth means.

So why is this doctrine somehow the first one to be tossed off the camel when Christians are trying to travel light across the desert of faith? Most of the problem is that those striving to prove Christian truth claims beyond doubt, known collectively as apologists, have used the virgin birth as a kind of trump card in a philosophical party game, and many of their exaggerated claims have done more harm than good.

So, for example, when I was a child I used to love a party game called bran tub where you'd dip your hand deep in a barrel of sawdust and search around and pull out a hidden toy. Christian apologists have used the virgin birth as a toy that proves the Old Testament is a barrel of prophecies that the New Testament fulfills. But this claim falls at the first hurdle. Today's text from Isaiah 7 doesn't say "virgin," it says "young woman." For Matthew to translate it as "virgin" makes a lot of sense in his understanding of who Jesus is—but it's hardly a straightforward fulfillment of prophecy.

To take another example, Christian apologists tend to develop the same "barrel of sawdust" approach to science in a mistaken hope that finding a useful toy after a long rummage somehow advances their claims. So, from time to time, you hear that certain mammals have the capacity to conceive offspring without male intervention, by a process called *parthenogenesis*. This is very interesting science but worse than irrelevant to the question of the virgin birth because the point about the virgin birth is not that Joseph *wasn't* involved but that the Holy Spirit *was*. There's obviously a serious scientific objection to the miracle of the virgin birth, but it seems to me that the response to that objection is not to search deep in the sawdust for obscure counterscience. The only response is to say science studies phenomena that happen repeatedly and predictably whereas Matthew is talking about an event that happened only once.

There's plenty more down in the sawdust barrel, let me assure you. Take the claim that the virgin birth proves that Christ was divine. This seems to come out of some kind of prehistoric rule book of how to be a god, in which we see that Zeus and Dionysius and their friends went in for sophisticated origins, so you can tell that Jesus is one of the big guys because he did some fancy footwork at conception too. The trouble is that a great many people, including Jehovah's Witnesses and many Muslims, believe in the virgin birth but don't believe in the divinity of Christ. So much for proof.

For all these mistaken claims and plausible counterclaims, the most fashionable objections to the virgin birth are the moral ones. These take two forms. One is to say, why does God waste his time doing unnecessary miracles like a virgin birth when he doesn't seem to have time for much more pressing miracles like ending war and transforming human suffering? It seems to me this kind of argument, while ostensibly based on compassion for those who suffer, is really based on anger and resentment against God for not being exactly the god we want all the time. Surely rather than try to reduce God to our size and our logic, the virgin birth should be something we try to receive as a gift rather than reject as an insult. The wonder of the virgin birth is not that God pulled off a great stunt or that he suddenly removed human suffering at a stroke, the wonder is that God became fully present among us by bringing humanity and Israel into full participation and friendship with him.

The other moral objection to the virgin birth is that somehow it degrades women, either because it's portrayed as a kind of sexual assault on Mary or because Mary is taken to be simply passive and meek or because Mary's virginity plays into a male obsession to see women either as virgins or as whores and to see sexual desire as a destructive phenomenon for which women are somehow to blame. I think the Church has to acknowledge that there is much truth in this moral objection. The way Mary has been used as a figure to diminish women is not a proud aspect of our Christian heritage. But while acknowledging the false ways in which the story has been used over the centuries, I would deny that the conception of Jesus by the conjunction of Mary and the Holy Spirit inherently degrades women. It is clear that it's a matter of joy for Mary, a development she actively embraces, and, given that the Holy Spirit is neither male nor female, there's no man in sight. And don't forget that Jesus must have spent his whole life under some kind of social stigma because of the question over his origins.

So Matthew gives us layer upon layer of meaning that Mary represents Israel in providing the human context in which God could become known in the world. Some objections to the virgin birth are mistaken. But others are significant. So to believe in the virgin birth will always be a matter of faith rather than of certainty. But I want to finish by drawing one final parallel between Israel's faith and ours.

Israel's faith was cradled in the manger of exile. Five hundred years before Christ, the people of God made the long journey to Babylon, and when they got there they had no place to stay. While in Babylon they remembered their sojourn a thousand years earlier in Egypt where, again, they had no place to stay. The early Christians remembered those two long journeys of their people—to Egypt and to Babylon—and how, both times, God's people had no place to stay, and God brought them home. But the early Christians reflected on two more long journeys. There was the journey of Mary and Joseph to Bethlehem. Again, no place to stay. And there was the journey of God in Christ from heaven to earth. But this, the biggest journey of all, was different. There *was* a place to stay. Mary was that place. Mary shows us joyous human hospitality for the miracle of God's activity.

In Babylon, Israel discovered that the God who had brought them out of slavery in Egypt was the very same God who had created the heavens and the earth. The savior God was the creator God. The name for the union of salvation and creation was Israel. The early Christians made this same discovery in reflecting on the coming of Jesus. They realized that God's decision to save us is written into the very fabric of creation. The conception of Jesus is an act of creation and at the same time an act of salvation. In other words, the place where salvation and creation come together is called Mary.

We make that discovery when we see the Greek word Matthew uses both at the start of today's passage and at the start of his whole Gospel: *genesis*. Sound familiar? Genesis. The Bible is the story of salvation, but it starts with the story of creation that we call Genesis. The Gospel is the story of salvation, but it begins with a story of creation that Matthew calls "genesis."

What that word *genesis* means is that *the conception of Jesus is the beginning of all things*. Not chronologically, maybe, but the conception of Jesus names God's decision never to be except to be for us in Christ—and that decision is the beginning of all creation, of all life, of all salvation, of everything that matters. And so we see that *creation itself is a kind of virgin birth* because it was creation from nothing, and it was brought about by the Holy Spirit. And *the virgin birth is a new creation*—or perhaps even the original creation—because it, too, is brought about in some ways out of nothing, by the action of the Holy Spirit, although this time, gloriously, with a woman at the center of God's action. We have been brought out of nothing to be made for relationship with God, and God has made a home among us to unite our hearts with his. Creation is a virgin birth. A virgin birth is creation. As we say in North Carolina, "How 'bout that?"

Maybe it's time believing in the virgin birth came back into fashion.

Notes

1. Isaac Watts, "O God, Our Help in Ages Past" in *The United Methodist Hymnal* (Nashville: The United Methodist Publishing House, 1989), 117.

2

Speaking the Truth about Faith

Sharing God

This is an example of an issue (evangelism) that is generally avoided by mainline Protestant preachers, with the result that their congregations are left to draw their own conclusions about how to reconcile the Christian tradition with current practice and expectations. The theme was suggested by the lectionary text for the day, Luke 5:1-11. The approach is to bring together scriptural exegesis, reflection on contemporary questions (in this case evangelism), and personal challenge. The three categories I set out in this sermon are highly significant for what I believe myself called to be doing at Duke (as I explain in the introduction to this volume). In this sermon, I adapt the argument set out in my book *God's Companions* about the priestly and prophetic roles of the Church. My intent is partly to make the traditions that are today restricted to one part of the Church—in this case, evangelism—once more accessible to the whole Church (see my similar treatment of the Holy Spirit in chapter 4) and partly to demonstrate what cultural assumptions Christians need to set aside in order to offer the gospel in a new era. As I often do, I convey a dense argument by organizing it in categories that can easily be followed. I then offer exegetical insights to reinforce the points made and to help the members of the congregation make the argument their own.

Many theologians, most famously John Calvin, have seen Jesus' ministry as rooted in identifiable Old Testament roles. They point out that Israel was led to God by prophets, priests, and kings. Thus Jesus was a prophet (especially in his life), a priest (especially in his death), and a king (especially in his resurrection).

When we turn to today's Gospel passage in Luke, the same threefold office helps us understand what is going on. Jesus exercises a prophetic ministry by offering words of compassion and hope, and calling on Peter, James, and John to respond to that message of hope. Jesus exercises a priestly ministry by depicting and embodying the life to which he calls his disciples, and he offers a kingly ministry by showing his command over the forces of creation in the extraordinary catch of fish.

Since I've been living in America I've discovered a number of words we don't use here if we are going to be welcome in polite society. One of those words is a ten-letter word that is my subject today. The word is *evangelism*.

We don't use the word because it seems arrogant to suggest we have a truth others don't have. We don't use the word because it sounds aggressive, insensitive, and coercive to imply that others must be more like us. We don't use the word, perhaps, because we are so often embarrassed by the failures of our own tradition that we hesitate to commend it wholeheartedly. We don't use the word because we simply don't like to be associated with some of the people who do. After all, who wants to be labeled as a cultural imperialist?

I want to suggest that we shouldn't stop using the word but that we must grow more careful about the way we do use it. The way to be more careful is to distinguish between three kinds of evangelism—what I'm going to call prophetic evangelism, priestly evangelism, and kingly evangelism.

Let's start with prophetic evangelism. *Prophetic* is a much-used word in the American church. What I understand it to mean is this: placing an individual, an institution, or a situation in the light of God's story. That means recalling that all people are made in God's image, that God has called us into a covenant relationship with him, that he has shown us his very self in Jesus, and that he will finally end the story by rolling righteousness down like a never failing stream. The prophet calls people to locate their identity and transform their conduct in accordance with this unique story. The prophet knows that we can't become a better world without needing to become better people. Thus behind every plea to end the death penalty or to improve treatment for factory workers or to change our nation's foreign policy lies a call to conversion, a call for those in authority to turn from their ways and live.

The prophet points people to God. When our docents show visitors around Duke Chapel they say, "Look at that window; look at the expression on Lazarus's face." The prophet says, "Look at that community, that's how God wants people to live," but the prophet also points out to the world that it *is* the world and that it *isn't* the Church. The prophet says the American Constitution is a fine thing, but it's not a part of the Bible. The prophet says that confidence in the legal system is a vital part of our culture but that it can't give you what Jesus says matters most, which is forgiveness and reconciliation.

Prophetic evangelism speaks primarily to those outside the church. The second approach, priestly evangelism, principally addresses those inside the church. It seeks to shape a personal and communal life that imitates the pattern of Christ's work. Such a form of life hopes to thrill the imagination of any who might come into contact with it. Priestly evangelism realizes that words are not enough. There must be actions to match. In today's Gospel from Luke 5, Jesus doesn't just call Peter and friends to follow him; he does something that depicts the transformation he is talking about. Saint Francis famously said, "Preach the gospel at all times: use words if you have to." Congregations aspire to become parables of the kingdom, which draw strangers and even enemies to wonder at the hope that is in these people's hearts, but priestly evangelism is not restricted to the congregation. By being rooted in neighborhoods and committed to unself-conscious lives of service, congregations come to form partnerships across faith and other barriers to "seek the welfare of the city" (Jeremiah 29:7) and to learn from others the "paths that lead to peace."

So priestly and prophetic evangelism aren't alternatives. They work together. Priestly evangelism is concerned with giving prophetic evangelism something to point to, with providing a kind of exhibit A to demonstrate what the grace of God can do. Prophetic evangelism is concerned with engaging the kinds of people priestly evangelism is often too timid or self-effacing to talk to. The priestly makes the prophetic less strident; the prophetic makes the priestly less complacent.

The third kind of evangelism is kingly evangelism. For most of church history, certainly since the fourth century, the church has perceived or been offered the prospect of rule, a significant or dominant role in the ordering of society. Such a prospect has always been tempting because it seems such an ideal vantage point from which to point to God's ways to maximum effect and to embody God's life to maximum extent. The prospect of rule has so often been so tempting to the church that it has seldom been resisted, but its effects have invariably been a disaster.

Within a hundred years of becoming the official religion of the Roman Empire in the fourth century, Christian identity went from being illegal to being obligatory. The church became voluntarily captive to an agenda that had little to do with prophetic witness to God's mercy or priestly embodiment of God's grace but everything to do with social control. When the Reformation made that social control problematic (because there were now several kinds of Christianity), few seriously considered giving up on the social control. Instead they found military or political means to preserve it. This was the Europe many early settlers in America were fleeing, and yet so many reproduced here the same kingly evangelism they had left behind. Meanwhile later, in Africa, so much damage was done in identifying evangelism with social domination by Western powers that it has taken the African church many decades to begin to repair the damage.

Let me be quite clear what I mean by kingly evangelism. I don't mean speaking the truth about God in public places, even in spheres of government. That's integral to prophetic evangelism. I don't mean seeking to create and shape institutions around a generous, hospitable practice of worship, learning, and service. That's a healthy outworking of priestly evangelism. What I mean by kingly evangelism is when Christians enforce conformity to what they perceive as Christian norms from people who are not Christians and have no desire to be. It's when what should be an offer, an encouragement, a gift, becomes an expectation, an assumption, a requirement. If the norms they were imposing were love, joy, peace, patience, kindness, and so on, then it wouldn't be a serious problem, but we all know it has never been like that. Instead history provides a litany of examples of how in the name of Christianity those with power have driven through social agendas that were distinctly lacking in goodness, faithfulness, gentleness, and self-control.

What's wrong with this isn't simply that it is undemocratic or unjust, although it sometimes has been. It's that it is deeply damaging for the church. It makes the church invisible because the church becomes simply a means to the end of a society pressed into a certain kind of social straitjacket. It discredits priestly and prophetic evangelism because those who can't or won't embrace the joy of God in Christ stop listening to any kind of evangelism once they get a sniff that it's really a mechanism for social control. And it's hard to blame them, because one of the most depressing features of kingly evangelism is that the living, dying, rising Jesus Christ tends to disappear out of the picture. For example, I'd have more sympathy with those people demanding that certain so-called Christian principles be taught in schools if those principles were "You must always strive to forgive those who have deeply hurt you" and "You must never give up the hope of reconciliation even when your people and another people have been in unequal or hostile relations for generations." Somehow we never hear about those kinds of principles, maybe because kingly evangelism is seldom really about much that resembles Jesus at all.

All these things have made *evangelism* a dirty word in polite society today. Kingly evangelism has been such a destructive force, still so much in fashion in certain quarters (and nowhere more so than in this country), that even faithful, devoted followers of Jesus Christ are in many cases reluctant to be drawn into the priestly and prophetic dimensions of evangelism because of the history of kingly excesses. The temptation is to go in one of two directions. The "prophetic" temptation is to maintain the evangelistic fervor but to take out the distinctively Christian elements of the story. Hence one shouts about peace, justice, and human dignity but goes quiet about Jesus. The Christian story of creation, covenant, Christ, church, and consummation is replaced by a story of how privilege and ignorance are replaced by progress and equality. The "priestly" temptation, on the other hand, is to disappear into secluded Christian enclaves, not harming anyone but not benefiting anyone either, burying the talent of Christian hope in the hillside of cultural inhibition.

So what's to be done? I want just briefly to draw out four lessons from today's Gospel to suggest how the Church may restore its confidence in priestly and prophetic evangelism and give the world more confidence that the church has no kingly ambitions.

Lesson One, Jesus already knew Peter, James, and John. His prophetic call was based on an existing priestly relationship. The time for sharing faith is almost always after a relationship of trust has already been formed. This means evangelism is as much about listening as it is about speaking. The evangelist must expect to be changed as well as to change others.

Lesson Two, Peter's immediate reaction in the face of Christ's majestic power is, "I am a sinful man!" We, the Church, must repent. We must repent of the ways our message has been distorted and not pointed to the glory of Christ. We must repent of the way our common life has disordered and been a poor example of the grace of Christ. Most of all, we must repent of the way we have claimed Christ's kingship as our own and distracted, damaged, and destroyed others in the name of godly rule. In particular we have to recognize that it seems impossible to many, perhaps most, Jews to hear the word *evangelism* without assuming it means coercive kingly evangelism because Jews have been exposed to so much of it so destructively for so long. I think it's hard to imagine a time in the foreseeable future where Christians can expect Jews to listen to any prophetic evangelism, except perhaps from those themselves born Jews.

Lesson Three, Jesus' analogy of the disciples becoming fishers of people makes us wonder about the nature of fishing. No one ever said you go fishing for the sake of the fish. Evangelism is not fundamentally undertaken for the good of those seeing and hearing (although that's always the hope) but for the sake of the church. It's not judged on whether it makes the church more populated but on whether it makes the church more faithful. A church that doesn't evangelize will disappear into platitude or subside into complacency.

Lesson Four, Peter, James, and John left everything and followed Jesus. The shape of the story is that they had nothing, then miraculously Jesus gave them far more than they needed, after which they were content to have nothing. What they discover in the story is that if you have Jesus and the abundant life he brings, you don't need anything else. This tells us that evangelism is serious business. It takes everything we are and everything we have, and the Jesus we share is not our possession but is always out in front, always beyond our domestication. One of many things wrong with kingly evangelism is that it seems to say, "You do all the changing. You need to become like me." Prophetic and priestly evangelism by contrast say, "He's the one I'm following. It has cost me everything, but it's more than worth it. Would you like to come too? You can help me, and maybe I can help you."

So as we read Luke 5 today, there's good news and bad news. The bad news is evangelism has become a dirty word in our culture, and it's the church's fault for allowing faith-sharing to get mixed up with an unhealthy desire for social control. It's a legacy that's going to take a long time to live down. The good news is that evangelism doesn't have to be a dirty word. There's nothing oppressive or arrogant or manipulative or imperialistic about striving to shape a community of worship, learning, and humble service and drawing attention to such a community and its source of life when others become curious. The real news is that, without evangelism, there's no church and there's no discipleship.

We just need to remember this simple lesson. The church is a prophet and a priest that points to a king. But the only king is Christ.

The Heart of God

This is a sermon for Orientation Sunday. The first-year undergraduates come to campus a little earlier in August than their upper-class colleagues, and the first big Sunday of the semester is focused on them. The text from the *Revised Common Lectionary* was Exodus 3. The real energy of this sermon comes in the second paragraph and the simplicity of the aspiration expressed there. This sermon is an attempt to locate the heart-searchings of the disoriented first-year students within the overarching story of God. It sets out to be very direct and full of humor, recognizing that on an occasion such as this it is an important pastoral service to give release to the listeners' nervous energy. Along the way it seeks to name many of the anxieties a new student may have about faith and social life in a new environment. It engages the suggestive idea of freedom and places freedom in the context of salvation. It concludes by affirming that the life of faith is fundamentally not so much about the believer as about God. The result is to raise the bar of expectation so that four years at university are retold as a wonderful adventure with God.

I'm talking today especially to those of you who are new to Duke. (I, you understand, have been here all of two weeks, so I'm one of the veterans.) To begin life at a university means to wear every item in your wardrobe for at least a few minutes during the first week; it means to go from being profoundly ashamed of your family to missing them desperately in the time it takes to cross the quad; it means to listen to an endless number of people telling you to be yourself and relax while inside you've no idea any more who yourself is and you're about as relaxed as a violin string.

Your family, friends, and former teachers will have all sorts of hopes for you. I have only one: that here you will meet God. Your new friends and new teachers will have all sorts of expectations of you. I have only one: that you open your eyes and come face-to-face with God. What does it mean to meet God? That is what Exodus 3 is all about, and I want to explore with you four dimensions of what it says to us about God.

The first discovery is that God has a name—and knows yours. Moses says, in essence, "People will ask, what is your name—what shall I tell them?" You know this kind of conversation: I was once in a restaurant when half of the great Liverpool soccer team of the 1980s walked in and sat down at the next table. I said, "You couldn't sign this menu, could you? Not for me, you understand, but for some of the kids in the youth group." Moses says, "Of course, I don't need to know your name, but a lot of people will, so you couldn't just tell me, could you?" And God says "I AM WHO I AM." Not your average name, clearly, but it tells us some very important things. God is personal. God isn't just a vague sense of meaning, a guarantee of some abiding truth, or a hearty feeling of well-being. God has a name, God has an identity, and God communicates with us.

There is a tendency in public circles to talk of God as if God were a grand if old-fashioned way of referring to noble ideals—"freedom, justice, democracy . . . Gohhdddd." In other circles, God is used as a kind of enormous number, somewhere way beyond a billion but just short of infinity—a bit like the way I used to address letters to my friends—37 London Road, Bristol, England, United Kingdom, The World, The Solar System, The Galaxy, The Universe—and then you could add Gohhdddd just after the universe. Or God becomes a word for a profound experience, the kind of thing you shout out when you make love or see the Grand Canyon for the first time. Gohhdddd. But this isn't the God who meets Moses. The God who meets Moses is a particular and personal being who loves to talk with us and who won't be pushed around by our categories. I AM WHO I AM.

The second discovery is that this communicating God won't take no for an answer. Moses says, "This is unreasonable. You're asking too much of me. I can't save a whole people. You're setting me up to fail, you're going to make me look ridiculous, I'm new to this, I'd never have enrolled in the Freshman Exodus class if I had known it would be this much work, I'm going to take you to the Dean, the Provost, the President, this is so unfair." God just raises an eyebrow, like an archetypal Clint Eastwood, and says, "We'll do it together."

Now in my experience when you join a new family or a new club—when you meet your boyfriend's parents, when you turn up at the first lacrosse practice, when you settle down for your first orchestra rehearsal, or when you enter the class called "Khaled Hosseini and Tom Wolfe as prophets of the new American Century"—whatever it is, you spend your time in one of two ways. Some of the time you're thinking, "I feel a fraud. I wonder if anyone will notice how nervous I am, how gawky I look, how pathetic are my social skills; how long till someone realizes I'm really here because I fancy the conductor, or that I've never read a modern American novel or that I have an eating disorder or that I'm a virgin. I'm lucky to be here: I wonder how long it will last." That's some of the time. But the rest of the time you're thinking, "Actually I'm not as spotty as that guy over there; at least I didn't emit an involuntary bodily sound like that geek beside me; and I got a decent grade for my first assignment. Actually I think they're lucky to have me here, and I'm beginning to get a bit bored of the company they've provided me with." Half the time we're not good enough for the university; half the time the university isn't good enough for us.

It's the same with God. Half the time we feel like trash, and we're astonished God hasn't yet wiped us off his hard drive; the rest of the time we're thinking, "I'm a pretty regular kind of guy, and that God's pretty lucky to have me on his team." Moses spends half his time cowering from God and half his time saying, "Go on, if you're so special, prove it." But what Moses discovers is that what he thinks of himself doesn't matter that much. God isn't that interested in what Moses thinks of himself. "I will be with you." That's all that matters. God wants us to believe in him, for sure, but what really matters is that God believes in us.

Moses discovers a third thing when he meets God. God wants to set him free. The book of Genesis begins with the central discovery that God is a creator God, that everything traces its source and purpose to him. The book of Exodus is a new beginning because here we discover that God is a liberator God who longs to set his people free. And that combination is still almost too much for our imaginations. We're used to the idea of a God who shaped the mountains and rivers, who made the tiny microbe and scattered the Milky Way. We're getting used to the God of protest, that when the downtrodden call for justice and the heartbroken call for mercy God is in their struggle. But the idea that the creator God *is* the liberator God, that God makes us this way because he wants one like us *and* comes into our lives to set us free—wow. It's not surprising it was too much for Moses: it's still too much for us.

God wants to set you free. God wants to do to you what he did to Moses: to dismantle your fears, foibles, and folly, to expand your imagination so you can take in the wonder of what God has in store for you, to give you a new job to do in God's strength not your own, and finally to make you a part of the way God is setting free all the oppressed peoples of the earth. This is why we go to university: the better to be a part of the way God is setting his people free. The greater your imagination, the greater your understanding may become of the wonder of God. The more skills you learn, the more confidence you may have in playing your part in this great tide of liberation. The better you know the world, the deeper your grasp will be of the subtle ways people remain in chains, in chains to family ghosts, in chains to sibling cruelty, in chains to addictive substances, in chains to consumer choice, in chains to sexual greed, in chains to small electrical devices we have to check every five minutes to be sure we're still popular.

So this is what Moses discovers when he meets God: God is a real being with a name, an identity, and a longing to communicate with you. God has a purpose for your life and won't take no for an answer. God's purpose is to set you free and to set you to work setting others free.

There's one more discovery. God begins his conversation with Moses by burning in a bush that blazes but is never consumed.

Here is a God who loves his people with a burning passion, but a passion that is never exhausted. Here is a love that is on fire, but a love that does not destroy. Here is a God who shapes that burning passion in such a way that it will catch our attention, bring us into relationship with him, transform us, and set us free. That is how God works in Jesus, but, long before, that is how God was already working in the burning bush.

God is on fire with love for you. That is Moses' fourth discovery. It's not just that God is a personal being, with an unshakeable purpose to set you free. More than that, the reason for the story, the dynamic at the heart of creation and salvation and Bible and church is this: God is on fire with love for you. This is the discovery that makes sense of all the others. The burning bush is not just some visual aid, some highway road sign advertising burgers or fries on a wayside griddle. Neither is it a warning of hell or a threat of agony for the unwary. It is a picture of the very heart of God. Moses discovered the truth at the center of the universe. God is on fire with love for you.

May you feel this fire today. May it draw you without consuming you, embrace you without destroying you. May it give you identity and purpose, and may it set you free. While you are at this university, may you catch fire with love for God that your heart too may blaze with love for people and with longing to set them free, until the time when, ablaze for God as God is for you, you become all flame.

The Son of God

This is a sermon for Christmas Eve and takes the text of John 1:1-14. It is not specifically directed at students, but at the "intelligent skeptic," the person dragged along to church a couple of times a year by an enthusiastic partner or friend. The hinge of the sermon is the sentence, "And that's why it's so ironic that Christmas is a season where it has become part of the annual tradition for the self-styled 'real' Christians to criticize everyone else for being so materialistic." I am affirming the skeptics in their misgivings about the overly pious, but this creates the opportunity to set right many of the assumptions of both the pious and the skeptic.

In this sense, the shape of the sermon is intended to reflect the shape of the Christmas story: God uses the foolish to preach to the wise. This a more challenging sermon than many are used to hearing on Christmas Eve because it seeks to take the theological and philosophical claims of Christmas seriously but to do so in such a way that no one should feel excluded from the conversation. It is fundamentally an attempt to bring together the "spiritual" and "worldly" celebrations of Christmas to enable disciples to live more integrated lives.

When I was at seminary I had a friend called Andy, who lived next door. Most days around four o'clock he'd knock on my door, interrupt me from my studies, and say "Whasssit all about then? You found out yet? Want a cup of tea?" One way or another, whether several times a day or in the face of the mundane or the tragic, most of us ask ourselves at some point, "Whasssit all about then?"

What most of us are searching for is some kind of logic. We'd like to know why the earth is so tiny and yet so huge. We wonder why a year is so short, and yet a day is so long. We want to know why there are so many languages and so little honest communication. We want to know what love is and how to have just the right amount of it. On our days of despair, we miss this sense of an inner logic to things, some thread that ties it all together. We have a name for people who can adapt easily to the logic life has taught them. We say they are people with common sense. We have a grander name for people who seem to have penetrated beyond the outer logic of things to some deeper, inner logic. We say they have wisdom.

When Saint John composed the Gospel that bears his name, he was bringing together two parallel ways of thinking. One was Greek philosophy. The Greeks spent a great deal of time reflecting and pondering this inner logic of things. It was the center of their quest for meaning and truth. By the time John wrote his Gospel, the most influential form of Greek philosophy taught that the logic of things, which was called the *logos*, was a kind of fate and that the role of humankind was to bring its will into alignment with that fate. Wisdom meant seeing everything, even suffering, as stemming from that same logic.

The second way of thinking was the faith of Israel. The Jews believed not in mindless fate but in a personal God. They believed that God had chosen them to be a particular example to other nations of what it meant to be God's children. Living in the eastern Mediterranean like the Greeks, they'd picked up words like *logic* and *wisdom*, and these words appeared in their Scriptures, but it wasn't clear how these concepts related to the God who had called them to be a people.

What John does in the opening words of his Gospel is to bring the traditions of Israel and Greece together and say that God and logic were as one from the beginning: "In the beginning was the Word." In the beginning was logic, the *logos*. There is no God who is known without rationality, meaning, and truth, and there is no logic that can exist outside the logic of God. It was logic that shaped God's creation of all things. John then tells us about a person called John the Baptist. This man called John did what prophets had done throughout the time of the Hebrew Scriptures: he used logic to point to God; in other words, he pieced together the common sense and the wisdom of the world to point out that there was a logic that went beyond human logic, what we could call the logic of God, or perhaps the "Word of God."

And then John the Gospel writer delivers his awesome summary in the most significant words in all of history, theology, literature, and philosophy: "And the Word became flesh" (John 1:14). The logic of God became an actual person. That which the great philosophers had taken to be inscrutable fate became tangible flesh. The great and mighty Yahweh, the one whom the children of Israel were warned they could not even set eyes on, came among us as a human being. The message of God became a man. What mattered became matter. Meaning became material.

And tonight is the night when we celebrate that most breathtaking moment. Tonight is the night when we recognize that the logic of the universe is embodied in a tiny, fragile baby. The whole life of God is organized, the whole shape of the universe is structured, the whole logic of creation is ordered for this moment: that God become fully present and in loving relationship with us in the person of Jesus Christ. So the Christian faith is not fundamentally a theory or an ethic or an institution: it's fundamentally about a person, the Word made flesh; and about a relationship between the logic of God and our haphazard logic, between God's faithful presence to us in Jesus and our wavering fitfulness in response. Christianity is the story of that person and that relationship.

But somehow the wonder of Christmas is just too awesome for most of us most of the time. We get the logic bit—the Greek bit—most of the time. We get the idea that there must be some kind of organizing principle, some inner logic that underwrites the universe. How else, after all, would we sustain the work of an institution like Duke University, whose engineering and science and humanities are all founded on the assumption that there is such a logic at the heart of things and that we can find it out through research and experimentation? We also, particularly in America, somehow get the God bit—the Hebrew bit—most of the time. We get the idea that there's some kind of personal being out there or up there, who we often presume has a particular interest in us and to whom we turn in times of sorrow or tragedy or fear, or simply when we're looking for a word that means big and important and something that really matters. And that's where we tend to leave it, with a rather distant personal being who underwrites the logic within all things. Culturally it's useful because it gives meaning without causing much offense. And spiritually it's comforting because it doesn't ask too much of our imaginations or contradict too many of our commitments.

But it's not Christianity. Around this time of year, if we get tired of the carols, sometimes we put on a song like "From a Distance." It was written by Julie Gold and has been covered by Bette Midler, Nanci Griffith, Cliff Richard, and a host of karaoke artists. You must know it. It gives a wonderful picture of what the world looks like from a distance: a lush and beautiful garden whose inhabitants live in peace and concord, with a benevolent deity keeping an eye on things. "God is watching us from a distance." Sounds beautiful. But is it Christianity? No, no, no, no, no, no, no. It misses the whole point of Christianity. God is not some distant idea so spiritual that he rises above the clumsy material of earthly life. God doesn't watch from a distance like some benevolent grandfather watching the children play at the bottom of the yard. God joins in! The logic of the universe becomes incarnate in an individual human being. The Word became flesh!

This is Christianity: not some set of disembodied ideals and noble values but the life shaped around the logic of God in a human form, at Christmas found in a tiny crying baby, on Good Friday found in a naked man hanging on a cross, on Easter Day found in the wonder of a man defeating death and opening the gates of glory. This is what we find difficult about Christianity— not its sense of the spiritual, not its sense of inner logic and its appeal to a personal God, for who could be against such reassuring things? No, what we find difficult about Christianity is its *materialism*, its claim that God took human, material form and lived and died and rose again clothed in and surrounded by the sheer material stuff of ordinary life. A God who is watching us from a distance is a God we can keep at a distance. A God who takes human form is a God who comes up close and personal, a God so close to us that we can never escape his grace.

That's why it's so ironic that Christmas is a season where it has become part of the annual tradition for the self-styled "real" Christians to criticize everyone else for being so materialistic. Presumably this is because beneath all the wrapping paper and the schmaltzy mall Muzak and the inflatable snowmen and the PlayStation 3 is some kind of "spiritual" truth that most people aren't getting. And what is that oh-so-spiritual truth? That truth is that the Word was made flesh; in other words, God is the biggest materialist of all, so much so that in Jesus God became material because the heart of his inner logic was for us to be his friends.

Let's stop trying to be more spiritual than Jesus. The spiritual message of Christmas is that God became incarnate—literally, God took on human flesh, God became material. And that means the way to celebrate Christmas is to become materialists too. Godly materialists. Godly materialists seek God in human form. Godly materialists are like shepherds roaming around Bethlehem looking for Jesus among single mothers and teenage parents and homeless people and those who live among farm animals. Godly materialists are those who remember Jesus' parents fled Bethlehem for Egypt, and so godly materialists are on the lookout for Jesus taking fleshly form among immigrants and refugees and those in fear of their lives in a new country. Godly materialists are those who remember the wise men traveled across the desert to find Jesus in a manger when they thought he'd be in a palace, and so they're always aware that discovering the fleshly Jesus takes patience, persistence, and humility.

Christmas is about God going to extraordinary lengths to be present and in loving relationship with a people who needed God but weren't at all sure they much wanted him. The way to celebrate Christmas is to go to extraordinary lengths to be materially present and to offer loving relationship to people who need God but aren't at all sure they much want God, to people who need you but aren't at all sure they want you. This is godly materialism: offering flesh to make friendships. Hugging those whom no one hugs, eating with those with whom no one eats, listening to those to whom no one listens, touching those whom no one touches, remembering those whom no one remembers, loving those whom no one loves. This is what God did at Christmas: this is what we do at Christmas. This is how we celebrate our material God.

G. K. Chesterton famously said that the problem with Christianity is not that it has been tried and failed but that it has never been tried. That's because most of the time Christianity remains just an idea, an idea about an inner logic, an idea about a personal but distant God. But Christmas tells us that Christianity is not just a comforting idea; it's a fleshly reality. God took human form. The Word became flesh. Christmas is about stuff, about the stuff of life, and about how God put himself at the very heart of the stuff of life, the material of existence. And we can celebrate that fact in every fleshly, material encounter we have, today and every day. Don't try to be more spiritual than Jesus. Don't decry people for being materialists because God's a materialist. Be a godly materialist. Make Christianity a fleshly business in the most earthy, ordinary, and human connections of your life. It's astonishing that God wants to be part of this material, human, earthy existence. But he was, he is, and he always will be. That's the good news of Christmas.

The Absence of God

This is another Orientation Sunday sermon, this time on the concluding verses of John 6. Again there is meant to be plenty of humor, but this time the mood is a little less festive. The sermon is really a lament for the times when faith is fragile and God seems distant. It addresses the issue by drawing the congregation's attention to how deeply rooted its faith actually is, more so than each might often realize. The discussion of the crocodile is designed as an engaging way of talking about desire. It emphasizes that God brings something that no other experience or phenomenon can emulate, but it does so in the context of straightforward honesty about the challenges and setbacks of faith. As with the sermon in response to Hurricane Katrina, when it came to the key words, "To know, know, know him is to love, love, love him / . . . / and I do," I chose to sing them, partly to make them memorable but also partly to affirm the mood of lament.

As fresh-faced young undergraduates, the incoming class arrives at Duke to be surrounded by role models. In freshman week, you can't move for Residence Advisers, level-headed seniors, campus ministers, student affairs staff, and faculty, all saying reassuringly, "Trust me." But I'm going to suggest one more role model for our freshman class: a crocodile.

In the story of Peter Pan, we meet a character called Captain Hook. Captain Hook's hand has been replaced by a hook, after he had an encounter with a crocodile. The crocodile enjoyed Captain Hook's hand so much that he has since been permanently on the lookout for the rest of Captain Hook.

I wonder whether you've ever tasted anything so good that you've spent the rest of your life trying to find that taste again. There's a story that's popular in Ireland of the man who is visited by a fairy godmother and granted three wishes. He didn't have to think long about the first wish. "I'd like a glass of Guinness that refills as soon as I drink it," he said. Sure enough, his wish was granted. After he'd enjoyed a couple of drinks and found the glass kept replenishing, the fairy godmother said to him, "Don't forget you've got two more wishes." The man looked at the constantly refilling glass and said, "I'll have two more of those please."

When you have truly found what makes your heart sing, there's no need to search or speculate about much else. The crocodile knew what he was looking for. Captain Hook's hand had tasted so good that it was worth spending the rest of his days seeking the rest of Captain Hook.

If you can relate to the crocodile, you can relate to the dynamics of John 6. The chapter begins with Jesus' feeding five thousand people, starting with just a few loaves and fishes. The people say, "We like the taste of that; we'll have two more of those please." Jesus says, "I can give you something more important than loaves and fishes," and the crowd says, "Bring it on." And Jesus then says these unforgettable words: "I am the bread of life. Whoever comes to me will never be hungry, and whoever believes in me will never be thirsty" (John 6:35). I can't hear those words without the hairs standing on the back of my neck and my eyes beginning to fill with tears. If you've drunk in those kinds of words, if you've tasted a little bit of the Jesus who spoke them, you've become a crocodile. You've enjoyed just a little part of Jesus, and you're going to spend the rest of your life looking for the whole of him.

This is the good news. When Jesus breaks bread, there is more than enough for everybody. Then Jesus lays down his life, and he himself becomes the living bread, broken for the life of the world. Yet even Jesus' death is not wasted, and his resurrection offers us the promise that we shall eat this bread with him forever. I think I'll have a little bit more of that bread please. I think I'll never get tired of that bread. I think that bread is all I'll ever want. Give me this bread always.

But the Bible would be a very short book if that were all there was to it. Almost straightaway, people begin to find reasons why they'd like a second opinion. John 6 presents us with two kinds of reasons, both of which are still very much with us. The first is, this Jesus is too ordinary. He's Joseph's son, you know, the one who graduated from Nazareth State University with a wood skills major and a GPA of 3.4. Played a couple of matches as a walk-on for the sailing team and did a bit in religious life, the usual stuff. We still find Jesus a little ordinary. A lot of us long for truly dramatic visions or experiences or adventures or discoveries. Extreme sports can give you stirring feelings. Drugs can give you amazing hallucinations. Other religions can give you exotic insights or profound wisdom. Jesus sometimes feels just too ordinary to be the key to everything. The universe is massive and staggeringly complex. Sometimes it does seem curious to say it all comes down to this solitary historical figure 2,000 years ago.

The second reason people walked away from Jesus is the opposite of the first. They said he was too far-fetched. He wanted too much from them. He was too demanding. "Yes, yes, yes," they said, "We buy into this 'eternal life' thing and we're cool about this 'you will never be hungry' deal, but couldn't you just lay off the heavy stuff about washing one another's feet and giving all your money to the poor? Can't you realize that in the modern world everything's relative—no promises last forever, no truth claims go much beyond rhetoric and some kind of bid for power, no one gets to have a monopoly on what's important?"

The two reasons why people turned away from Jesus in Capernaum are pretty much the two reasons why people turn away from Jesus today. For some people, Jesus is too plain ordinary—a simple historical figure cannot bear on his shoulders the destiny of the whole world. They say why not just accept he was an exceptional human being and have done with it. For others, Jesus is too plain *extra*ordinary—they say Christianity is all very well but it does expect too much. "Allow me to make sure my appearance is perfect, allow me to get my achievements secured, allow me to get my affluence beyond any danger; now, yes, Jesus is quite a person and one day I must get around to thinking about the questions he asks of us."

Every Christian knows what it means to think and feel these things some of the time. Many of us can look back on days, weeks, or years when other things seemed more important or truer than Jesus. Maybe you are in one of those periods right now. But I want to remind you to be a crocodile. Remember the taste. Remember the joy. Savor the words, "I am the bread of life. Whoever comes to me will never be hungry, and whoever believes in me will never be thirsty." And just go heading off, slowly, methodically, relentlessly, having had a taste of Jesus and wanting to enjoy the rest of him. Be a crocodile.

Jesus squares up to the twelve disciples in today's Gospel and says, "Are you turning away too?" Think about this powerful moment. If the disciples leave now, what becomes of the rest of the New Testament? Who witnesses the crucifixion, who meets Jesus after the resurrection, who founds the first churches, who writes the Gospels? It's one of those cliffhanger moments in the Bible when everything hangs on the answer to the question. Peter swallows deeply, looks into Jesus' face, and says, "Lord, to whom can we go? You have the words of eternal life" (John 6:68). You're the only show in town. When you've seen what we've seen, discovered what we've discovered, shared what we've shared, tasted what we've tasted—nothing compares to you. Anything else is absurd.

You could call this the doggedness of belief. It's the stubborn conviction that the Jesus who said, "I am the bread of life" *is* the life of the world, that whoever comes to him *will* never be hungry and whoever believes in him *will* never be thirsty, even if that person couldn't care less at the moment. Four years ago, I was the priest of a socially disadvantaged parish in the east of England. Sometimes it seemed no one cared less about Jesus. I can remember Sunday mornings when I would arrive at 9:30 for the 11:00 service, set out the chairs and everything else, and wait. And sometimes at 10:55 I would still be the only one there, longing for someone to come and share the bread of life. I would wonder what I was doing, holding out for Jesus when no one seemed to want him. And these words of Peter were the words that kept me going: "Lord, to whom can we go? You have the words of eternal life." You're the only show in town.

There are many words for the attitude that Peter's words represent. Doggedness is one. Stubbornness is another. Faithfulness sounds a bit better. Perseverance sounds a bit more pious. But the real word is *love*. This is what it means to love God—to follow him around like a crocodile seeking the best meal ever. Because it's about love, the pop artists have had plenty to say about it. Take these lyrics written by Phil Spector and recorded by the Teddy Bears in 1958: "To know, know, know him is to love, love, love him / . . . / And I do."

I want to close by saying some words directly to those of you who are new to Duke. You've come to a university that prides itself on teaching you how to think, and sometimes what to think. We have some wonderful thinkers at this university, and I trust you will grow by learning how they think and by thinking alongside them. But this morning, you have come to a place that wants to show you who to love. And I say to you: Love Jesus. Love him with all your heart and mind and soul and strength—the way he loves you. There may be times in the years ahead when some of your thinking comes to question some of your loving. Don't panic. Look around you now: you can see hundreds and hundreds of people who have been through the same thing. You may for a time find Jesus just too ordinary or for a time find Jesus just too demanding. Don't despair. You'll be in good company.

My prayer is that at the end of your time at Duke you'll be even hungrier and thirstier for Jesus than you are today. You'll have asked yourself many times, "To whom can we go?" You'll have had a look at a good number of those to whom we may turn, and you'll have made an informed judgment about who really does have the words of eternal life. I anticipate that the more you learn about the atom or wave theory or calculus or the civil rights movement or the nineteenth-century novel or sustainable economic growth, the more you'll long for the food that never perishes, the drink that never runs dry. And it's just possible that on your last night at Duke, you'll remember the crocodile, and chuckle, and find that you are quietly singing to yourself, "To know, know, know him is to love, love, love him / . . . / and I do."

3

Speaking the Truth about the Bible

Identifying Discipleship

If my theological priority is to encourage the congregation by showing there is no issue that cannot be illumined by theological engagement, my exegetical priority is to display the riches that the Bible has to offer to the contemporary church and its disciples. This sermon followed the reading of Mark 5:21-43. Rather than assume the Bible is simply for the individual in devotion, simply for the activist in mission, or simply for the congregation in worship, I sought to describe all three in a lively way. If I had had longer, I might have explored a fourth dimension: the scholar in the academy. The sermon seeks to bring all the resources of the contemporary academy to the layperson, showing the transition from the assumptions of historical criticism to the possibilities offered by rhetorical and narrative criticism, but to avoid jargon and show how fruitful these methods can be. The sermon was originally entitled, "How to Read the Bible in Three Dimensions."

The Bible is not a book. It was not written to be a book. Instead, it is a collection of scrolls, long stretches of papyrus that were kept in a dry place, treasured by faithful communities, and brought out to be read aloud on special occasions. Those who translated the Bible into Latin started producing copies as huge books. But it was not until the sixteenth century, with the invention of the printing press and the Reformation (which sought to put the Bible into the hands of the common people in their own languages) that the phrase "my Bible" meant anything. The Bible became a book.

I want today to look at Mark's intertwined stories of Jairus's daughter and the woman with hemorrhages. I want to show why it matters *where we are* when we're reading the Bible. I'm going to look at three places where we might read these stories and what they might mean when we read them there. I'm going to start with you, sitting alone, at home, with the Bible on your knees. We could call it the Reformation position.

When you read the story by yourself, you are struck by the parts that resonate with your experience. You notice Jairus. Here is a wealthy and powerful man, a major figure in his synagogue. He has no hesitation in coming before Jesus. He's the kind of person who calls up the president of the university and assumes the president can give him an appointment the same day. But the big thing in his life is that his beloved twelve-year-old daughter is sick and close to death. He falls at Jesus' feet and begs Jesus to help. When we read this, it puts us in touch with our own deepest needs. Is this how we pray to Jesus? Fall on our knees at his feet and beg? Even if we are a big wealthy guy? Maybe we should. And then we notice a very different approach. The woman with hemorrhages isn't the kind of person who assumes Jesus will clear his calendar to meet her. She doesn't think she's worth a moment of his time. She comes up from behind him. She touches the hem of his cloak. So one person comes to meet Jesus face-to-face, demanding his attention, and another comes round the back, not daring to meet his eye. Which way do you come to Jesus? Do you come through the front door or through the back door? Which way do you pray, through articulate requests or silent touch?

Then we notice that, though their approaches are very different, both people find health—or salvation, which is the same word in Greek. The first thing Jairus says to Jesus is, "My little daughter." The young girl comes as a member of a loving, supportive family. By contrast, the woman with hemorrhages comes before Jesus alone, and in fear and trembling. She has no support team, no network of love and trust to help her through her life's struggle, but Jesus says to her that same word, "Daughter." In other words, "If you've no family, be a part of mine." Hear Jesus saying that: "If you've no family, be a part of mine."

We notice both stories involve touching, but it's a different kind of touching. Jesus touches Jairus's daughter: he takes her by the hand. But in the case of the hemorrhaging woman, it's the other way round. She touches him. This shows us something wonderful.

With Jesus, it's not just that he touches us—moves us, restores us, inspires us, forgives us, heals us—it's that we touch him—he is moved, affected, touched by our gesture, our neediness, our faith. He feels the power go out from him. He notices the difference made in his life by a poor, outcast, friendless woman. He notices us.

Look at the subtle difference between the prayer of Jairus and the prayer of the woman. Jairus's prayer is for his daughter; the woman's prayer is for herself. Both prayers lead to healing and salvation. We see the faith of Jairus and the faith of the woman. We know nothing about the faith of the young girl. The young girl is saved by the power and love of Jesus and the faith and persistence of her father. Does that not inspire us, as we shape our intercession list? Many of us who worship at Duke Chapel live comfortable lives. We don't face the social exclusion that the woman with hemorrhages experienced every moment of the day. We may face personal torment, like the agonizing illness of a young daughter, but when we look at this story, we know we are Jairus. Well, let's *be* Jairus: let's get on our knees and plead with Jesus for the sake of the desperate and those at the gate of death; let's keep faith, even when the bystanders tell us it's hopeless; let's discover that we and the socially excluded are as one when we come into the presence of Jesus. That's why the Prayers of the People are perhaps the most important thing we do at Duke Chapel. They are the great leveler that brings a Jairus church to its knees before Jesus.

As you see, there's a lot in this story to read from the Reformation position, home alone. But I want you to read this story again in a different place. This time we're going to read it in a group, a group of Christians active in costly relationship with one another, committed to friendship with the poor and in witnessing for justice among the powerful. We could call this reading the Bible in the Liberation position. What do these people see in this story?

They see a story about how different everything is depending on whether you have money or not. Jairus is a big shot, a leader, a rich man. He gets straight to Jesus. Five times Mark mentions the crowd in the first few verses of this story: they are surrounding Jesus. But Jairus gets put straight through to the boss. The woman with hemorrhages, by contrast, is about as excluded as you can get. She had been bleeding, and thus was unacceptable in public, for a very long time. She had spent all her money on quack doctors, who had only made her worse. She was poor, sick, unclean, and alone. Not much has changed. In this country today, to be sick means to be poor, more often than not, and to be poor means to be sick, all too often. To be poor and to be sick means to be heavily dependent on a strong network of family and friends, but if you had a strong network of family and friends you quite probably wouldn't be poor, or at least not as poor as this; and quite possibly if you weren't this poor, you wouldn't be sick. The woman with hemorrhages is in a vicious circle of poverty and ill health.

This isn't just a story about wealth because Jairus is also in despair. Jairus has a problem that money can't solve. In this country, such a problem is becoming an increasing challenge to the imagination. You could say that America's goal today is to get to a point where there is no problem that money can't solve. When we come up against problems that money can't solve, we become very angry, and we assume someone must be criminally to blame. We are a Jairus culture, but we are sometimes slow to learn what Jairus learns in this story. Poor Jairus finds that his wealth can't protect him this time. His daughter dies and becomes ritually unclean, just as the hemorrhaging woman is ritually unclean.

And that brings us to the heart of this story from a liberation perspective. It is fundamentally a story about purity and about sex. The young girl is twelve years old, the age when formally she becomes a woman and can be married. The hemorrhaging woman is a woman for whom sex and childbirth in this culture are impossible. Jesus comes into physical contact with both of them. It ought to make him ritually unclean, but astonishingly it doesn't. Rather than their impurity making him impure, the opposite is the case: his holiness makes them holy. As with Jesus' relationships with Gentiles and with sinners, it is Jesus' holiness, not their impurity, that is contagious.

Think for a moment how revolutionary this is. Purity is fundamental to rhetoric about sex: you just have to reflect on the importance of a white dress at a wedding. When we panic about what teenagers get up to at parties or at college, we probably think less about whether they are becoming loving, trusting, forgiving people than about whether they are losing their purity and becoming somehow dirty. Purity is also fundamental to the rhetoric of race:

in America of all countries, the famous melting pot of cultures, there is even now a pernicious myth about some kind of purity that must remain unsullied by mixing races. Absurd as the idea of a pure race is, cocktail of historical and biological nonsense as it may be, it nonetheless has a powerful hold on the imagination.

But these stories show us that, with Jesus, purity is not a possession we're in constant danger of losing but a gift we're constantly offered the possibility of receiving. Holiness is infectious. Purity is contagious. It's impossible to overestimate what a revolution this is to the way most people are taught to think about religion. Jesus has so much love, so much healing power, and so much compassion that when the unclean woman gets anywhere near him she's infected with holiness. That's surely what we long to be as Christians. Not frightened shadows who fear relationship because it might make us dirty, but people so full of compassion and truth and longing for justice and gentle understanding that holiness infects everyone who comes anywhere near us. We long for contagious purity, the purity of forgiveness and healing.

For many people, the Bible has become a book that they read alone or perhaps in a study group regularly or occasionally. As I hope I have shown, there is so much to find in the Bible when we read it this way. But there is a third place in which reading the Bible is vital and life-giving. This is the place that gives the Bible its third dimension, and that is in church, as we are doing now. We could call this reading the Bible in the liturgical position.

What does it mean to read the Bible in church? It means to read the ministry of Jesus in the Gospels in the company of the stories of God's relationship to Israel recorded in the Old Testament and in the company of God's destiny for the church set out in the remainder of the New Testament. It means to set the reading of scripture in the context of an ordered series of liturgical actions that seek to embody Jesus' life, death, and resurrection and to shape our character to reflect that saving action of God. It means to set our own hearing of the Bible story alongside the way other, perhaps very different, people hear the same story so the whole people of God can be enriched by the diversity of his creative purpose.

When we read the stories of Jairus's daughter and the hemorrhaging woman in church, this is what we find. We realize that the number twelve is vital to both halves of this story. The young girl is twelve years old, and the woman has been bleeding for twelve years. The number twelve is a shorthand way of referring to Israel because Israel was the nation of twelve tribes, so here is a story about a dearly beloved daughter of God called Israel. This dearly beloved daughter is sick, indeed close to death. She is desperate, and those faithful people in Israel call on God to save her. And Jesus comes into the story to save Israel, to restore her to health and relationship and well-being. When he appears, he is thronged with the overwhelming breadth and depth of human need. Rather than seeing this as a distraction, he points out that the poor, the outcast, and the unclean are at the very heart of God's story and that they are the children of God, too. Then he resumes his ministry to Israel, faces derision, misunderstanding, and mockery from the bystanders, and raises Israel to life from the point of impurity and death.

The story of the young girl and the bleeding woman are intertwined with one another just as the story of the rich and the poor, of Israel and the Gentiles, of the righteous and the sinners, and of the pure and the outcast are wrapped up in one another. There is a "correct" way to come to Jesus, and the synagogue leader comes the correct way; but there is also a direct way to come to Jesus, and the uncouth crowd, in the form of the bleeding woman, comes the direct way. This is telling us that we can never simply see the profound neediness of the world outside the context of God's overall relationship with Israel and the church, and one can never tell the story of God's love for Israel and the church without remembering that the poor and the outcast are at the heart of that story.

So reading the Bible challenges each of us to a three-dimensional faith: alone, together, and in the Church, in devotion, in action, and in worship. The stories of Jairus's daughter and the hemorrhaging woman show us what it means to come to Jesus, front door or back door. They show us what it means to pray for ourselves and for others. They show us that Jesus transforms both the rich and the poor. They revolutionize our understanding of purity, showing us that in Jesus it is holiness that is wildly contagious. They offer us the whole history of salvation, placing God's love for the poor at the heart of his love for Israel and the church. This is what it means to read the Bible in three dimensions. Now it is time for us to live in three dimensions.

Identifying Jesus

This sermon follows the text Luke 1:26-38. It is exegetically perhaps the most ambitious of all the sermons in this volume. Here I use the full theological and hermeneutic resources I have available, offering a new reading of a familiar text that places it firmly in the context of Israel. I find myself returning over and over again to the significance of Israel to Christian theology and ethics, and I am increasingly persuaded that the airbrushing-out of Israel from the Christian tradition arises from sinister motives. In another setting, perhaps one of the English parish churches where I served for many years, I would have asked the congregation to enact the Mexican Wave as I announced the accumulation of the parts of the story, but that is not the Duke Chapel way, and a distraction in style would have seriously reduced the impact of the content in this context. The Sunday before Christmas is a time for beginning to let the light of Christmas intrude on the twilight of Advent, and this sermon was intended as a rousing introduction to the celebration of the great festival.

In 1986, the soccer World Cup was held in Mexico. You wouldn't remember it because, sadly, the United States didn't qualify. The tournament is best remembered for bringing to a world audience that communal activity beloved of stadium crowds, the Mexican Wave. The phenomenon is said to have begun at a Californian baseball game in the early 1980s, so you could say it's another product that America outsourced south of the border. In the United States, it's just called "The Wave" because calling it a Mexican Wave might affect the balance of trade figures. These days, the crowds who start a Mexican Wave tend to be either very young or very bored. Looking at the crowd we've got in the chapel today, you're clearly not very young, so if I see a Mexican Wave starting I'll know you're getting pretty bored and I'll get the message that it's time I gave the sermons a rest for a while.

I want you to imagine the Old Testament as a Mexican Wave and that each major development in the story is like that wave reaching a new part of the crowd, with its own cheer. If this were an elementary school, I'd now divide you into sections, but I'm going to resist that temptation and leave it to your imagination. The way the first half of the Old Testament is written, it's all leading somewhere. The cheer gets louder and louder until it reaches a climax.

It starts with the story of God in Genesis 1 saying, "Let there be light." Let's call this part number one. This is a story about the sheer power of God's word to bring something out of nothing. God just says the word and says, "Let it be," and it is. And all is good. Then there is the story of Adam and Eve. We'll call this part number two. This is a story about how God longs for us to be his friends and how he makes everything possible for us to keep that friendship, but it is also a story about how first the woman, then the man, disobey God.

The next major part of the story, which I'll call number three, is the story of Abraham, Isaac, and Jacob, sometimes known as the patriarchs. God calls Abraham and says that Abraham will have as many descendants as the stars in the sky and they will be a blessing to all peoples. God changes Jacob's name to Israel and renews the covenant with him, even though Jacob isn't much of a role model.

Then the next part, which we'll call number four, is Moses, when God intervenes in history to set his people free and gives them the law to make them holy, set apart for him. Moses is the key intermediary between God and his people, the one who gives the law to Israel. The law, written on two stone tablets and kept in a container known as the ark of the covenant, which itself was kept for a long time in a tent, that law was considered the embodiment of God's presence among his people and his commitment to them.

And number five, which we could call the climax of the Mexican Wave, where the cheering gets loudest and the waving becomes more frenzied, is David. In David, all the vital pieces seem to be in place. Israel has the Promised Land and is safe within its borders. It has a capital city, Jerusalem, conquered by David. It has a king, and a king to be proud of. It certainly appears to have God's favor. This seems to be the right time to crown that favor by building a Temple, a true place for the glory of God to dwell among his people. Nathan the prophet and David the king have a debate about this, and the conclusion seems to be that the house that God is establishing is not a physical one but a fleshly one, not one built out of cedar wood but one that follows David's descendants.

There is a new departure in this story in 2 Samuel 7. No longer does God say, "If you keep my covenant I will be your God." There are no longer any ifs in this relationship. "Your throne shall be established forever," says God in 2 Samuel 7:16. No small print. No get-out clauses. You know what they say about the traditional breakfast of fried eggs and bacon? The chicken's involved, but the pig's committed. Well, here, God moves from being a chicken to being a pig. God is committed to Israel. No ifs or buts. That's what makes today's Old Testament passage so important. It really is the high-water mark of the whole story.

Then it all falls apart. After David's son Solomon dies, the kingdom splits, foreign powers invade, and Israel goes into exile, losing land, city, king, Temple, and most of all, favor. Catastrophe. After the return from exile there is a hint of a new era, which we could call part number six. This is the era of prophecy when, in the books that lie toward the end of our Old Testament, prophets began to talk of one coming who would change, restore, transform. But the prophets fell silent, and the Mexican Wave fizzled out. The Israelites were back in their land, back in their city, and even had a new Temple, but it wasn't the same because they had no king, no David.

That's where Luke's Gospel begins. Imagine that the Mexican Wave doesn't take place in a stadium with seating all around but in an arena more like the football stadium here at Duke, where it goes about four-fifths of the way around. The Wave dies out as the prophets fall silent, right where the seating comes to an end. And Luke begins at that very point, with the promised—you could say prophesied—birth of a new prophet, a big time prophet proclaiming some mighty big news. Just imagine those lethargic sports fans, amongst whom the Wave had died out, just stirring to their feet, almost in slow motion. Section six is rising to its feet, but it's not yet clear whether it's a yawn or in celebration.

But wait, look, here, later in Luke 1:28, here are these words, "Greetings, favored one." Sound familiar? We haven't heard anything about being favored since the time of David. And look, there's more about David. "He will be great, and will be called Son of the Most High, and the Lord God will give to him the throne of his ancestor David" (Luke 1:32). This is beginning to sound like section five rising to its feet. Suddenly we're hearing "forever" language again, for the first time for a thousand years. There is section five, the David section, beginning to stand and wave their hands and cheer. The Wave is reviving and going back the way it came.

Section four, the Moses section, is a bit more subtle. You need to think about what Mary is doing in this story. She is being summoned by God to play a vital role in giving to Israel the complete embodiment of God's renewed covenant. There is an exact analogy between what Mary is doing and what Moses once did. The signal is the word *holy*: "Therefore the child to be born will be holy" (Luke 1:35). *Holy* is a word that points directly to Moses because the whole concept of holiness comes into the Bible with Moses, beginning at the burning bush and centering on Mount Sinai, and the declaration that Israel will be a holy nation just as YHWH is a holy God. So the Mexican Wave is now really on the move: the prophets are coming back, David is coming back, and Moses is here too.

On to section three, and now it's getting pretty exciting. If you remember the movie *The Blues Brothers*, you'll know how the two boys go round up all their old mates, the oldest swingers in town, and mutter the stirring words, "We're getting the band back together." That's what's happening here. Luke's account of the annunciation is going back through the main sections of the Old Testament getting the band back together. Next in line is section three, the patriarchs. Gabriel says, "He will reign over the house of Jacob forever, and of his kingdom there will be no end" (Luke 1:33). This new initiative from God embraces not just the hope of David, the hope of a new king; not just Moses, the hope of a renewed covenant that puts the heart of God back among his people in a way that had not been since the ark of the covenant was lost in the fall of Jerusalem six hundred years before Mary was born; not just David, not just Moses, but God's initiative embraces even Jacob; in other words, it goes back to the beginning of Israel's story, back to the blessing to every nation and the call of Abraham himself.

But there's even more. The crowds are now making a terrific noise because section two is on its feet. Section two, you'll remember, is the garden of Eden and the story of the woman who disobeyed. Here we are again at a crucial moment in the biblical narrative, and this time the woman says yes: "Here am I, the servant of the Lord" (Luke 1). Think about what it means to be a servant in the ancient world. It means to live in the house of your master and be around him all the time. So the friendship with God that was abrogated in the garden of Eden is well on the way to being restored. Mary is now a member of God's household. Mary has taken a step beyond the scope of Israel. This is a step that goes back even before Abraham. It is a step toward the reconciliation of the whole of humanity with God.

We haven't finished yet. There's one more section to rise to its feet. Genesis 1 itself. "Let it be with me according to your word," says Mary in Luke 1:38. This is the language of the great creation story. Not only does Mary say "Let it be," the same words God uses to speak the world and the universe into being; she also refers to "your word," the Word of God, the word God spoke and the heart of his creative power. If there should be any doubt that this is a reference to the first creation story, look at the way the baby is to be conceived: "The Holy Spirit will come upon you, and the power of the Most High will overshadow you" (Luke 1:35). Here is a direct echo of those early verses of the creation account. I once heard a lector read from the first words of the Bible, "the earth was formless and void, and darkness covered the face of the Abbess." It certainly changed the way I think about convents. But even that lector got the next words right: "the spirit hovered over the face of the waters." And that's what happens here: the Spirit hovers over Mary, and there is a new creation. The story of the coming child embraces not just the reconciliation of the whole of humanity but the renewal of the whole universe. We're talking about a new heaven and a new earth. The whole of the Old Testament is about to be fulfilled in this young woman's womb.

So each one of the six sections of the great stadium has risen to its feet in a growing crescendo of joy and celebration. Gabriel's message to Mary is an announcement without precedent. The angel is saying, *This is a new David, God wholly committed to us with no ifs or buts. This is a new Moses, God fully embodied among us and setting us free, making his tent with us and being visible among us. This is a new Jacob, a promise that does not depend on our worthiness or unworthiness but extends to all God's people as a blessing for every nation. This is a new Adam and Eve, a new obedient relationship that sets right God's friendship with the whole of humanity. This is a new creation, the Spirit once again hovering as the word of God makes the impossible possible and brings light out of darkness.*

Luke is telling us that wherever we stand in the stadium, it's time to rise to our feet. We may be standing in the prophets section, down in the dumps and longing for a sign or a leader to promise a change in our fortunes. We may be in the David section, deeply aware of promises that sounded so sweet but seem to have been cruelly broken, and lost in regret or bitterness or nostalgia. We may be in the Moses section, longing for God to be close to us, to give us clear instruction and a sense of what it means for us to live a holy life. We may be in the Jacob section, knowing how foolish and cruel we can be and wondering if God has any patience or mercy left for us. We may be in the Adam and Eve section, wondering if one terrible mistake has ruined our whole lives. We may be in section one, the creation section, wondering what is the meaning of the universe and troubled by the way humanity is squandering the heritage of the planet's equilibrium.

Whichever of the six sections we're in, we may have had plenty of reasons to stop the Wave, but Gabriel's words to Mary shake us out of our boredom, our sadness, and our skepticism. Behold. The Lord is with you. It's time to stop yawning, stop crying, stop worrying about being embarrassed, and get up on your feet, celebrate, and wave your arms high. For here is a new king, a new presence, a new covenant, a new friendship, a new creation. God is coming home to us and bringing us home to him.

Identifying Science and Other Faiths

This sermon adopts an approach I enjoy using: letting the story create a structure for investigation. In this case, the story is Matthew 2:1-12. The structure it creates is a threefold one: what the magi learn in the East, what they learn in Jerusalem, and what they learn in Bethlehem. The central argument is that science can get the believer to Jerusalem but only revelation can get the believer to Bethlehem. Because the sermon follows the structure of the story, the argument does not seem contrived, and meanwhile there is no separation between exegesis and application—the two blend into one. A longer sermon might well have been able to explore the other locations lurking in the background of the story—Nazareth and Egypt, with their own lessons to offer. The sermon concludes with an affirming yet challenging call to locate oneself in the story, lest the earlier discussion seem too cerebral.

Those of you who know the story of *The Lion, the Witch and the Wardrobe* will know that in England we love Turkish Delight. The advertisement for Fry's Turkish Delight always surrounded the sweets with mist, and spice, and potion, and scimitars, with a hint of distant onion-shaped domes and sands in the distance. It ended with the words "full of Eastern promise." The story of the coming of the wise men is just like this: full of Eastern promise. I'm going to look at the story in three parts: what we learn in the East, what we learn in Jerusalem, and what we learn in Bethlehem.

So, first: what we learn in the East. We learn that God makes himself known to those outside the regular circle of his acquaintance. What is particularly striking is that not just Gentiles are among those who come to worship Jesus. According to Matthew, these magi are the first to worship Jesus, after he is born under the very noses of the political and social and religious elite of Israel, none of whom seem remotely aware of what is going on. Those who make the discovery are the outcast and unclean in Luke's account (that's to say the shepherds) and the distant and uncircumcised in Matthew's account (that's to say the wise men).

The wise men are able to see the working of God in the world in the form of the unusual star. Here we learn on the one hand that God does work by shifting the heavenly furniture around and, on the other hand, that outsiders to the faith may have at least as much access to this kind of action of God as the regulars. The beginning of this story is a clear statement that God does communicate with those who are seeking God, even if they are separated from the company of the faithful by distance or tradition. God doesn't belong to the Christians today any more than God belonged to the Jews in the time of Herod.

I once went on holiday in North Africa and traveled down to the Sahara Desert. I took a camel ride out to the dunes and hired a guide to come with me. When I reached the viewpoint I wanted, I got out my camera and composed classy photographs of the scene from various angles. Just as I began to think about moving on, I realized that I hadn't seen my guide for quite a while. Walking around a corner I spotted him, semiprostrate, making his prayerful oblation to God. I was humbled, realizing how I and he had respectively spent the previous fifteen minutes. How could I say that this man was far from the kingdom of God?

Now we move to the second part of the story: what we learn in Jerusalem. What we learn in Jerusalem is the other half of what this story tells us about wise sages from other traditions. The first part of the story told us that the magi could discover God in their deep and earnest searching and their honest and faithful researching. This second part of the story tells us that although their careful conclusions did indeed bring them to Israel, their journey took them to Jerusalem and not to Bethlehem. This, perhaps, epitomizes what this story has to tell us about what we might call the faith of the non-Christian. The faith of the non-Christian may indeed get to Jerusalem, but it is not clear that it gets to Bethlehem.

In other words, one can logically deduce that there must be a God and that God is revealed or in some way disclosed by his activity in creation, in the stars, in minute details, grand designs, or curious accidents. These investigations may indeed get one to the God of Israel centered on Jerusalem, but the whole point of this story is to demonstrate that the God fully revealed in Jesus Christ is centered not on Jerusalem but on Bethlehem. It is only when the wise men got to Jerusalem and were shown the scripture that directed them to Bethlehem that they moved from being general God-fearers to worshiping Christians.

So this story shows the possibilities but also the limits of a faith that is founded on personal discovery, investigation, and, to use a contemporary word, science. There's a great deal in the news about matters such as intelligent design, and there is always interest in whether one can ever prove the existence of God. While these matters will always be interesting for Christians, it's hard to see how they will be our primary concern. The reason is that they can get us to Jerusalem but not to Bethlehem. In other words, they can get us to a point where we conclude there may well be some kind of a God who could perhaps be personal and probably has some kind of purpose for the universe, but they never get us anywhere the God Christians actually believe in, the God who longs to be in relationship with us, the God who in Christ lays down his life for us, the God who at Christmas comes among us in tiny, fleshly, vulnerable form as a human baby.

We learn two other things in Jerusalem at this second stage of the story of the wise men. The first is that if we are to be leaders, as these Eastern sages were leaders of their own people, then we have to be able to recognize when we have made a mistake. To admit you have made a mistake is not the equivalent of saying you realize you are a terrible leader and should be replaced; it is to affirm that learning is a feature of every organization and that as a leader you are a part of that process of learning, not exempt from it. We live in a culture that has a myth of the leader-savior who takes over an institution and does no wrong. We need to say this is nonsense. It is not only factually untrue but has little to do with the Christian emphasis on forgiveness and reconciliation. Life isn't about not making mistakes but about what you do when you've made them.

I once heard a leading British politician interviewed on a radio phone-in program. He had opposed the British entry into the European Community in the 1970s, but twenty years later he became a European Commissioner, one of the bureaucrats who run the whole European enterprise. The caller said to him, "How can you represent an organization you used to oppose?" The politician replied, "When I realize I have made a mistake, I change my mind. What do you do?" The caller had nothing to say. The wise men realized they had made a mistake. Three times in this story they show both leadership and humility. They do so at the beginning by setting out across many miles to find the new king. They do so at the end by bowing down to worship him. But perhaps most of all, they do so in the middle by accepting they have made a mistake.

The last thing we learn in Jerusalem at this second stage of the story is that Jesus is a political threat to the status quo. This is a particularly important thing to remember a few days after getting very excited about a tiny baby. Just as parents a few days after a birth realize it's not so much about the wonder of birth and tiny life as it is about dirty diapers and sleep deprivation, so do Christians a few days after the birth of Jesus remember it's not so much about the timeless beauty of Christmas as it is about the way Jesus turns the world upside down. Turning the world upside down makes the mighty who are on their seats very angry.

It may help to have a bit of background on the manner in which the Roman emperor ran his empire. Rather than dominate and overrun his subject people, he creamed off perhaps 5 percent of the population to act as retainers. These people would get significant benefits in terms of wealth, prestige, and power. All that was required in return was loyalty to Rome. Thus at the time of Jesus' birth, Rome could afford not to rule Judaea directly. Instead it simply controlled the people and raised taxes through a vassal king, Herod the Great. Herod died shortly after Jesus was born, and his sons had neither his authority nor his skill; so following Herod's death, Rome took to administering the province directly, by installing a governor.

Nonetheless, the Roman governors kept on the various hierarchies of retainers to act as intermediaries between them and the largely Jewish population. And well they might, for, as my father-in-law is fond of saying, "Why keep dogs and bark yourself?" The Roman governors had found a formula that meant they could control the province and meanwhile acquire considerable wealth for themselves, not by suppressing the people with military force but by manipulating those among the population who sought wealth, prestige, and power. That is why in the Gospels there are only occasional encounters and confrontations with Roman authorities and soldiers. Most of the disputes are with Rome's stooges, those whose obedience to Rome demonstrated they had lost all sight of being God's holy people. At Jesus' birth in Bethlehem, these stooges attempt to wipe out any hint of a rival king. A generation later in Jerusalem, they finally get their man.

And so to the third and last part of the story of the wise men. What do we learn in Bethlehem? Already we have learned a lot. We have learned about the way God reveals himself to those outside the Jewish and then Christian faith. We have learned about the difference between science and revelation. We have learned about how leaders make some of their most important gestures when they are prepared to acknowledge they have made a mistake. We have learned about the ways in which the birth of Jesus constituted a political threat to the Jewish and Roman authorities in Jerusalem. Finally, in Bethlehem, we learn where we fit into the story.

Our place in the story of the wise men is to be the star. The star gains the wise men's attention. The star continues to point toward Bethlehem even when the so-called wise men think they know better and head toward Jerusalem. The star hovers over the place where the baby lies. Our role is to be this star.

It may be that you are trying to bring up a family and encourage wayward children to take seriously the claims of the Christian faith. It may be that you are striving for justice to be brought into the courtrooms or legislatures or public spaces of this town, state, this country, or much further afield. It may be that you are acutely aware of your powerlessness to change the flow of events, to persuade a partner not to break up the family or to encourage a friend not to give up on a long cherished dream. Your role is to be the star. Your role is to live your life in such a way that people are interested not so much in you as in the joyful reality to which your life is pointing. Your role is to keep pointing to that joyful reality even when those whose attention you long to attract are busy or uninterested or exploring blind alleys. Your role is to be still pointing to the joyful reality when the moment comes when those whose hearts are restless in Jerusalem start wondering again about where the joyful reality is really to be found. Remember, stars shine most brightly at night, when the way forward is hardest to see.

Your role is not to be Jesus, miraculously changing everything forever. Your role is not to be Herod, deeply threatened by any development that might shift you from the center of the story. Your role is not even to be the wise men, seeking truth on the edges of God's ways. Your role is to shine the light on the humble but transforming reality of Jesus, God with us. Whether people, wise or foolish, notice your shining light is not necessarily your department. Your department is making sure that light is shining, making sure that everything you think and speak and do is pointing to the transforming humility of the manger. Your job is to ensure one thing: that you're a star.

4

Speaking the Truth about Discipleship

Joining Jesus' Body

This sermon was preached at a service of baptism and confirmation, on the text Acts 10:44-48. It is an attempt to speak straightforwardly about the Holy Spirit to a congregation who might fear that such a subject means trouble. It is also an attempt to place baptism and confirmation in a healthy relationship to one another and to the Christian life as a whole. This is a project that is not often done. Confirmation services are often occasions for a pep talk for those being confirmed rather than a consideration of the nature of confirmation itself. Outside of confirmation services, the subject is almost never brought up. The subtle agenda in this sermon is to make the Acts of the Apostles accessible to the whole Church, rather than simply to the charismatic movement, and thus to help the whole Church enjoy elements of the tradition often restricted to one of the parts. It was originally entitled "Receive, Believe, Become."

It is sometimes said there are two kinds of people: those who believe there are two kinds of people and those who don't. There may, nonetheless, be two kinds of Christians: those who hear the words "Holy Spirit" and think, "Praise the Lord, at last someone's talking about the power of God" and those who hear the Holy Spirit and think, "Help—I'm going to be expected to make strange noises or speak in tongues or sing music that doesn't have four part harmonies or go to services that last over two hours."

After the four Gospels, we have in our Bibles a book called the Acts of the Apostles. In some ways it might be a little easier to understand if the four Gospels were renamed the Acts of Jesus and the Acts of the Apostles were renamed the Acts of the Holy Spirit because the Holy Spirit is principally about one thing and that thing is making Jesus present. The Holy Spirit makes present the Jesus of the past and the Jesus of the future. The Jesus of the past is the Jesus who was born, was baptized, was tempted; who called disciples, taught, healed, and confronted those who oppressed the people of God; who was arrested, tried, tortured, and crucified; and who was raised, appeared to many, and was taken up to heaven. The Jesus of the future is the Jesus who will come again and who will unite heaven and earth in a new realm of joy and perfect freedom, in an unending relationship with God the Trinity, in which all creation will worship God, be God's friends, and share God's banquet.

The Holy Spirit makes the Jesus of yesterday and the Jesus of forever present today in regular and surprising ways. The regular ways are in the sacraments of baptism and Eucharist, in the practice and experience of personal and corporate prayer, in the reading of scripture and in gestures of mercy and kindness. The surprising ways are in the wise words of a stranger, in the apparent disaster that turns out for the best, and in the way God seems to work through the most surprising people.

Because a lot of Christians are rather scared of the Holy Spirit, I'm going to set out today three key words that express how the Holy Spirit works in the Church and, particularly, how that work relates to baptism and confirmation.

The first key word is *receive*. This is a word that makes it absolutely clear that God is not our poodle. The Holy Spirit comes according to its own calendar, not ours. The Holy Spirit is not a puppy that we can train to walk or sit or lie down when we shout the right command. A former colleague of mine spent some time serving a church in Ghana. Like North Carolina, Ghana gets very hot in the summer, but unlike North Carolina there's not much in the way of air-conditioning. It so happened that the church didn't have enough money to put any glass in the windows. This had the advantage that it let a bit of air in. The only problem was that there was also quite a strong breeze, so they found that when they brought papers into the church the papers blew all over the place. Eventually they decided that having the wind blowing through the church was intolerable, so they got together enough money to put glass in all the windows. The result was simple. The wind blew the roof off.

The lesson is that you can't dictate how the Holy Spirit will act in the church. The Holy Spirit is to be received, not grasped. It sets its own agenda. A number of years ago I was the pastor of a small congregation in a socially disadvantaged part of eastern England. A visitor came to the church one Sunday, and since we had only fifteen or so adults, we were quick to spot a visitor. This visitor had a rather fixed notion of what it meant to be a church, and he found our service very confusing. My sermon followed the scripture passage very closely, but we had candles on the altar. We sang simple choruses led by a guitar, but I wore traditional vestments. The visitor stayed afterward and asked me, with a frown on his face, "What kind of church *are* you?" I thought the best thing to do was to ask Huggy. Huggy had been part of the church for several years. He was of mixed race, had held a number of jobs and known a good bit of unemployment, and was universally recognized, partly because he weighed more than three hundred pounds. I said, "Hey, Huggy, our visitor wants to know what kind of church we are." Huggy paused to think and then said, "Open to God."

Open to God. That's what it means to receive the Holy Spirit. Huggy's church didn't have preconceived ideas about what God could or couldn't do. The Acts of the Apostles takes us through a series of encounters with people who challenge what the Holy Spirit can or can't do. First there's the Ethiopian eunuch, a Gentile man mutilated but in the wrong way. He comes into the kingdom. Then there is Saul, a Pharasaic persecutor of Christians. He comes into the kingdom. Then there's Cornelius, a Roman commander who was both a Gentile and a member of an army that kept the Jews from restoring God's promise. Cornelius too enters the kingdom. The only issue is whether the believers can keep up with the wildfire work of the Holy Spirit.

This is the scary ministry of the Holy Spirit—dramatic, sudden, surprising—something we can only receive. But there's another kind of ministry of the Holy Spirit, for which I use the word *become.* Once there was a rich man. He met and fell in love with a young maiden. She was lovely in form and lovelier still in character. He rejoiced when he saw her. Yet he grieved also, for he knew that he was not like her. His face was hideous, and his heart was cruel. He considered how he could win her hand.

Eventually he hit upon a plan. He went to see a mask maker. He said, "Make me a mask that I shall become handsome. Then, perhaps, I may win the love of this noble young woman." The mask maker did as he was bid. The man was transformed into a handsome figure. He tried hard to summon a character to match. It was sufficient to win the heart and hand of the fair maiden, and they were married. Ten years of increasing happiness followed, but the man knew he was carrying a secret. He sensed that true love could not be founded on deceit. He had to know if his wife really loved him, if she loved the man behind the mask. So one day, with a heavy heart and trembling hand, he knocked a second time on the mask maker's door. "It is time to remove the mask," he said. He walked slowly and anxiously back to his home. He greeted his wife.

To his astonishment, she made no comment nor showed any untoward reaction. There was no scream, no horror, no revulsion. He searched for a mirror. He looked—and saw no ugliness but a face as handsome as the mask, a face so different from his original face. He was amazed and overjoyed, but bewildered and confused. He ran back to the mask maker to find some kind of explanation. The mask maker said, "You have changed. You loved a beautiful person. You have become beautiful too. You have become beautiful through loving her. You have become like the face of the one whom you love."

The Acts of the Apostles is not just a story of the sudden, spontaneous acts of the Holy Spirit. It is also the story of how people who love Jesus become like Jesus, the story of the slow formation of a community of Jew and Gentile, slave and free, men and women, oppressor and oppressed, of the slow becoming of the body of Christ out of a people who had known so many dividing walls of hostility. The Holy Spirit is about receiving but also about becoming.

In the tradition of churches that practice infant baptism, we call the receiving part baptism and the becoming part confirmation. Of course, baptism is a sacrament the parents think about long and hard, but tell that to the baby. The baby feels the full force of the sudden action of the Holy Spirit—splash. The young people standing before us today didn't decide to be baptized. Baptism was something they simply received, but they did decide to be confirmed. Confirmation names these young people's consent to a long process, already begun and not yet finished, by which the Holy Spirit enfolds them into the body of Christ, in which they wear the mask of Christ's beauty but have not yet fully become like the face of the one they love. Baptism and confirmation belong together because they reflect the two contrasting aspects of the work of the Holy Spirit—the sudden and the gradual, the part God does alone and the part in which we have a significant role to play, the kind we simply receive and the kind we slowly become.

I have left something out. I've left out the bit between the sudden and the gradual, between receive and become. It's a bit of both. It has the "be" of become and the "eive" of receive. Believe. Believe in Jesus Christ, crucified and risen, incarnate on earth and ascended into heaven, Son of God and Son of Man. If *receive* means being tossed a set of football clothes, *believe* means putting them on, and *become* means running out with the team onto the field to play. The Holy Spirit, remember, is always and only about one thing—making Jesus present. Whether it's dramatic, like the roof blowing off in Ghana, or gradual, like the man's face changing under the mask, it's always about Jesus. That means it's always about faith. Faith is a gift, coming from outside us; we can't make it happen. That's the *receive* bit. But faith is also something we grow into, by being surrounded by people whose lives show us what God can do. That's the *become* bit. Receive, believe, become.

The Acts of the Apostles teaches us not to get too hung up about the order. Sometimes the receive bit comes first, as on the day of Pentecost. Sometimes the believe bit comes first, as in today's story about Cornelius's household. Sometimes the become bit comes first, and people seem to be living like Christians when they have neither been baptized nor had a dramatic experience. Don't worry about the order. Too much angst has been created over the order. There's no definitive order.

But do ask yourself, "Which one of these do I find most uncomfortable? Do I find the receive part the difficult bit because I like to be in control of God and don't like surprises? Or do I find the believe part the hard bit because I like drama and I sense I'm growing into a community of passion and transformation but I find the details about Jesus elusive? Or do I rather find I stumble over the become part because I like what Jesus has done for me, but I struggle to turn that into participation in a community of discipleship?"

Whichever part you find uncomfortable, do two things today. Have the grace to thank God for the gift of the Holy Spirit he *has* given you and for the fruits that the Spirit has borne in your life. And don't be too shy to ask for those gifts that the Spirit still has in store for you. Ask for them now. Gifts. Faith. Fruits.

People of God, receive the Holy Spirit. Receive. Believe. Become.

Making Jesus Smile

I had a lot of fun with this sermon. It concerns Mark 2:1-12. In this sermon, I am seeking to do a number of things. I am certainly encouraging and displaying figurative (that is, not simply historical) readings of the Bible, particularly in this case the Gospel healing miracles. I slowly build up to the key exegetical point—that the roof signifies the boundary between earth and heaven and that the stretcher bearers reenact the incarnation. I then cajole the congregation into a playful state of mind, seeking to change the disciple's aspiration from averting God's wrath to making God laugh. Then I do a serious trawl through the Bible and contemporary public life to provide overwhelming evidence that this is exactly who God is and what God wants. Finally I come back to a second exegetical move, concerning what I describe as *intercalation*. It is an ambitious sermon exegetically, but the intention is to hide the academic moves in humor and a host of accessible examples. It asked too much imagination of one or two members of the congregation who hastened to point out to me that there is in fact no record of Jesus smiling in this story. Which is, of course, true—but true in a different way from the truth I am seeking to communicate here.

You'd think that reading the Bible would be the simplest thing, but in fact it's something we need to learn how to do. The story of the healing of the paralytic in today's Gospel is a good example. If you're used to the gospels, you hardly notice the miraculous healing. Jesus seems to perform so many healings that you almost glaze over. Huh, another healing. There's also a controversy with the scribes. But Jesus is like Dick Cheney—never out of the papers, always getting in trouble—so that seems no big deal. Your attention strays to the less regular parts of the story, the link between healing and forgiveness, and the curious entry through the roof. If you'd never read the story before you'd immediately think, "Who's this guy who can heal people, just like that? And why doesn't everyone give him a standing ovation?"

Learning to read the Bible means avoiding both these extremes: neither reading wearily, for the hundredth time, and saying, "It's just a healing," nor pretending it's the first time and saying, "It's a *healing*—everybody!" Learning to read the Bible means paying close attention to the details of the story and then setting those details in the context of the whole story and style and sweep of God's dealing with the world. So, let's look at the details of this story and then finish by seeing how those details fit into God's whole way of dealing with the world. Let's start with the four friends carrying the paralyzed man on a mat and digging through the roof to get to Jesus.

Think for a moment about the drama of this event. There are a number of barriers between the paralyzed man and Jesus. One is the man's paralysis. You could say the paralyzed man represents Israel in the time of Jesus' ministry. Does Israel need healing; in other words, does Israel need cleansing of the demon Rome, the paralyzing and crippling power of the alien invader, and does Israel need a Messiah to drive out the Romans, finally to end her internal Exile and restore her to fully functioning health, to stand on her two feet again and "go home" like the man at the end of the parable? Or does Israel need not healing but forgiveness; in other words, are Israel's problems not so much external as internal, in separation from God, and is Israel's paralysis less about the Romans than about trying to operate while still estranged from God? This is a question at the very heart of the New Testament.

Another barrier between the paralyzed man and Jesus is the huge crowd of people, so dense that the stretcher bearers can't get through. And at the center of the crowd is this infuriating group of scribes who seem to jump on Jesus every time he does something that sets people free. Why are the scribes so cross? Well, think about who the scribes are. They are the Conference, Diocesan, and Presbytery administrators, the Divinity Faculty, the Christian journal editors, the people who made a healthy living out of religion. People like me, in fact. These people muttered about Jesus; they set up emergency meetings, wrote strongly worded editorials in jour-nals, raised points of order at faculty councils, and whispered that the budget for next year could still be subject to change—all the kinds of things administrators do when they are riled. This story looks like a healing issue between Jesus and the paralyzed man, but behind it lies a control issue between the scribes and the crowd. This is the first time in his Gospel that Mark mentions the crowd, but they get another thirty-seven mentions, so they're pretty important to the story. It was the scribes who controlled whether sins were for-given and debts released. This was the source of their social power. If Jesus was going to go around announcing that sins were forgiven, the social power of the scribes would be over. Jesus isn't just setting the paralyzed man free; he is setting the crowd free as well.

So paralysis, crowd, and scribes are all barriers. The last barrier is the roof itself. The roof is the easiest barrier to deal with: it takes neither authority nor miraculous power but imagination and elbow grease. This is a story describing how the gospel takes away every barrier between us and God and how, when we finally come into God's presence, we are set free. The four friends symbolically remove the "roof"—that which stands between earth and heaven. Then Jesus, the heavenly Son of Man, takes away all that might paralyze us in every other way. The whole scene is a summary of Jesus' mission to Israel. Jesus transforms the paralyzed man from a burden into a carrier, from a person carried on a mat to a person who carries a mat, a person who is now in a position to carry oth-ers on that mat. The story shows us that if we bring people to Jesus, Jesus will do the rest.

Let's look a little closer at what the four stretcher bearers do in coming through the roof. Jesus is "down there," apparently out of reach, and they break through the barrier to reach him. You could say they *break through the barrier and come down from heaven to earth.* Think about this gesture. It's a very significant one. Why? Because the whole gospel is about *Jesus* breaking through the barrier between God and humanity and coming down from heaven to earth, and here the four stretcher bearers do pretty much what Jesus did. They imitate Jesus. What is Jesus' reaction? Jesus is charmed. You can imagine him smiling, a kind of wry, ironic smile, when he realizes these friends are imitating him. Think of a pro-fessor smiling when she recognizes one of her stock phrases in her graduate student's dissertation, even though the graduate student hadn't put it there on purpose. Think of a father smiling when he sees his daughter flick her head back or open her eyes slowly and sweetly, just like her mother does but entirely unconsciously. Think of a sophomore receiving a Valentine's card and chuckling as he reads a private joke that only makes sense in the light of a Valentine's card he sent to the same person exactly a year before. "Ah, you remembered; you understand; I don't need to explain to you," says Jesus.

These four stretcher bearers have come from heaven to earth. They have reenacted the incarnation. Jesus smiles. Nothing gives him greater pleasure. A few years ago there was a great campaign with its own slogan and bumper sticker, WWJD: "What would Jesus do?" This initially sounds like a short cut guide to doing the right thing, but it became open to ridicule. The reason is that it tries to ask how we get out of a problem without considering how we got into it. For example, I may be a high-flying international financier who has borrowed stocks from fifteen different countries simultaneously and suddenly there's a market crash and I'm trying to offload my stocks, and I wonder whether I should have a social conscience and offload the ones from the poor countries first or whether I should keep myself in business by selling for a better return in the rich countries. "What would Jesus do?" is a bit of a silly question because it's hard to imagine Jesus getting into such a crazy situation in the first place, given what he said about keeping promises and building houses on rock and how he spent most of his time with the poor. An Irish friend of mine likes the story of the man who was asked for directions to Waterford and said, "Ah, if I wanted to go to Waterford, I wouldn't start from here." That's the problem with WWJD—nine times out of ten you wouldn't start from here. YWSH. (You Would Start Here.) What finally did it for WWJD was the revival of interest in the shaggy dog with the goofy detective assistants. The interesting question, it turned out, really was, WWSD: "What would Scooby Doo?"

Rather than using Jesus as a kind of safety valve, an extra gallon of gasoline we can draw on when we forgot to fill up the tank one morning, we should be thinking like the four stretcher bearers, "What is the kind of gesture that makes Jesus smile because he recognizes himself in it?" We can all think of these gestures pretty easily, especially when they have been captured in memorable photographs. Think of Tiananmen Square in Beijing in 1989 and that man who stood still while four tanks rumbled mercilessly toward him. Jesus recognizes himself in that gesture because he stood still before the rumbling power of Roman oppression and the Jerusalem authorities' plotting and the relentlessness of human sin. Think of the twin towers on September 11 and the firefighter clambering up the stairs while thousands hurtled downward to save their own lives. Jesus recognizes himself in that firefighter because he, too, put his life at stake to rescue us from the wreckage of the Fall. Think of the sinking of the passenger ferry the *Herald of Free Enterprise* in Zeebrugge harbor in 1987 and the man who lay between two broken corridors and made himself a human bridge at the cost of his own life so that others could walk over him to safety. Jesus recognizes himself in that man because he too is a bridge that others cross to safety at the cost of his own life. And think of Gordon Wilson who forgave the IRA for blowing up his daughter Marie at Enniskillen in Northern Ireland in 1987. Jesus recognizes himself in this gesture because he too at the moment of his death said, "Father, forgive them; for they do not know what they are doing" (Luke 23:34). These are all gestures that are disarming because Christ so instantly recognizes them. None of those making the gestures thought what they were doing was a big deal; like the four stretcher bearers breaking through the roof, these people put their inhibitions and personal anxieties to one side and simply did what needed to be done. These people made Jesus smile because their actions resembled his.

The four stretcher bearers in today's gospel join a great company of those in the gospels who disarm Jesus by imitating his life in ways that make him smile. Think of the poor widow who put two small copper coins into the Temple treasury in Jerusalem in the story often known as "The Widow's Mite." Jesus commends her because she gave everything she had to the Temple, the place where Jews became reconciled with God; likewise, Jesus gave everything he had to reconcile the Jews with God. Think of the Syro-Phoenician woman who tells Jesus that "even the dogs under the table eat the children's crumbs" (Mark 7:28). She reminds Jesus that there is a place in the kingdom for Gentiles. She's the only person who ever changes Jesus' mind because she accepts the humiliation of speaking the truth, just as Jesus later does in Jerusalem. Think of the woman who anoints Jesus at Bethany. Jesus commends her because she alone realizes he is soon to die and because her extravagance imitates the extravagance of God's love for us in him.

So those are some of the details of the story: the paralyzed man is like Israel, forgiveness breaks the stranglehold of the scribes, the descent through the roof is an imitation of Jesus' descent from heaven to earth, and the man's raising to health is a foretaste of Jesus' resurrection. I said I would finish by putting those details into the context of the whole story of God. So here goes.

I want you to notice the shape of this story. The paralyzed man is brought to Jesus; Jesus breaks off to have it out with the scribes; and then Jesus turns back to the paralyzed man and heals him. In other words, the scribal controversy about forgiveness is sandwiched between two halves of a story about healing. The technical word for sandwiching is *intercalation*. Mark's gospel does it repeatedly. The story of the healing of the woman with hemorrhages is sandwiched or intercalated between two halves of the healing of Jairus's daughter. The death of John the Baptist is sandwiched between the sending out of the twelve disciples on mission and their return. Jesus' cleansing of the Temple is sandwiched between his cursing of the fig tree and his return to find the fig tree withered. Jesus' anointing by the woman at Bethany is sandwiched between the chief priests and scribes searching for a way to arrest Jesus and Judas's coming to the chief priests to seal the deal. Peter's denial of Jesus is sandwiched between Jesus' faithfulness before the Jerusalem authorities and his faithfulness before Pontius Pilate.

What these intercalations do is to illuminate one story in the light of the other. In the case of the paralyzed man, the intercalation makes clear that you can't think about healing and forgiveness independently of one another. Forgiveness names the fundamental resolution of our estrangement from God, but healing names those aspects and consequences of sin that take longer to repair. Forgiveness requires confession, but healing needs intercession. Forgiveness removes the poison, but healing restores the body. Forgiveness ends the war, but healing makes the peace. To those who have found healing, this story says, "Great—but is it founded on forgiveness?" To those who have found forgiveness, this story says, "Great—but has it issued in healing?"

Intercalation is more than a literary device. It is the whole perspective of the gospel. Mark's gospel is written during a time window, and that window is between Jesus' disappearance at the end of the gospel and his reappearance at the end of time, between his first coming and his second coming, between his resurrection and our resurrection. Our lives, the life of the church, are sandwiched between God's mighty acts and can only be understood in the light of them. The way to live our lives, personally and corporately, is to follow the four friends of the paralyzed man—to perform gestures that imitate the outside parts of the sandwich. These gestures may be dramatic, like the anointing, or almost invisible, like the widow's mite; they may be messy, like digging up the roof, or argumentative, like the words of the Syro-Phoenician woman. Whatever your gesture is, it will be known by two things. It will be instantly recognizable by Jesus and by everyone who knows him, and, most of all, it will make Jesus smile, knowingly, wryly, ironically, and wonderfully.

Living Jesus' Life

This sermon was preached on the First Sunday in Lent to a very large and expectant congregation. I followed the temptation account in Mark, which is exceptionally brief. It is a good Sunday for a sermon that sets out some kind of manifesto. I owe the insight about Mark's three interwoven stories to Ched Myers's incomparable commentary, *Binding the Strong Man*. Like many of my sermons, I am trying at the same time to address major social issues, re-present the Bible as a thrilling word for today, and offer some categories within which the members of the congregation can locate themselves in their attempt to follow Jesus. Once the categories—in this case disciples, poor, and authorities—are familiar, I can then move to the more challenging theological couplet: the temptation of wanting to have God without Jesus or wanting to have Jesus without God. Again like many of my sermons, I am assuming that one cannot have doctrine without justice or justice without doctrine, but I am trying to display this in such a way that the congregation comes to take it for granted.

When I was a child I had a picture book of the Lord's Prayer. On the page for "Lead us not into temptation" there was a picture of a boy with short pants looking over his shoulder to check for his mother's reappearance while his hands ransacked the cookie jar. I think that picture, and others like it, can shape our whole idea of what temptation means. It characterizes temptation as quick, furtive, and rooted in greed. It leaves us feeling dirty, fearful, ashamed, and with a little bit of indigestion. I think there's rather more to be said about temptation than that.

What I'd like to do today is describe the story of Mark's Gospel, then go on to show how Mark's story is our story, and finally to show how Mark's story redefines what we think of as temptation and how we are to overcome it.

Mark's story is, in fact, three interwoven stories. First of all, there is Jesus' creation of a new community based on the messianic hopes of his preaching. He calls around him twelve disciples and commissions them to spread the fire of his kingdom. The disciples falter and stumble, out of fear of the cross, lack of imagination, and cold betrayal. But in Mark's account of the resurrection, there is promise of a restored community in Galilee.

The second story is Jesus' mission to the crowd, the teeming mass of poor and oppressed whom Mark mentions thirty-eight times in his gospel. This is a ministry of healing, exorcism, and liberation through story, announcement, and gesture. On Palm Sunday, the crowd seems to have taken up the cause of liberation, but by Good Friday they have chosen the terrorist Barabbas instead.

The third interwoven story is Jesus' confrontation with the powers that held Israel in a stranglehold. One by one Jesus takes on the Pharisees, the scribes, the Herodians, and the Sadducees. He dismantles their authority and challenges their control, but eventually the veil of pretense is pulled aside, and behind it emerges the real power in Israel, the power that toys with all other powers—the iron fist of Rome. It is the nails and wood of Roman execution that finally destroy Jesus, only for him to dismantle even Rome's control over life and death.

These three stories, of disciples, crowd, and authorities, are interwoven in Mark's gospel like three strands in a rope. Each finds its climax in the account of Jesus' passion. The three stories in the end constitute one story. And that story is the sending of Jesus by the Father, crystallized in the Father's words at Jesus' baptism, "You are my Son, the Beloved" (Mark 1:11), epitomized in the Father's words at the Transfiguration, "This is my Son, the Beloved" (Mark 9:7), and climaxing in the centurion's words at the cross, "Truly this man was God's son!" (Mark 15:39). Jesus' intimacy with the disciples, his mission to the crowd, and his confrontation with the authorities are all dimensions of his being at the heart of God.

So that's the story of Mark's Gospel—three stories united in one. But I said that I was going to show how this story is our story. So listen carefully: you'll notice our story divides into the same three strands as Mark's story—discipleship, issues of poverty, and conflict.

First, we reflect Mark's gospel by being part of a group of disciples. When we become a Christian, we are called into intimate relationship. We may already have close family ties, and our call to follow the man from Nazareth may intensify and strengthen these existing relationships, or it may test and challenge them. But either way, we are called to make new, close, and accountable relationships with members of Christ's church. These may earn the name of friendships; on the other hand, they may never become friendships, just stubborn, intractable, and sometimes downright irritating relationships with people who remind us to do stubborn, intractable, and sometimes downright irritating things like show up at worship on Sunday and tithe our income and pray for our enemies. During the Lenten season, we take stock of our Christian life. When we take stock of our intimate life, we must ask, "Am I part of an accountable group or network of relationships? Am I part of a 'group of disciples' in any meaningful sense?"

Second, we reflect Mark's Gospel by attending to the crowd, by being in relationship with the poor and oppressed. There are all sorts of ways to do this. I guess the characteristic Duke way would be to invent a diluting agent that meant vaccines didn't need to be refrigerated and so more than the current 50 percent of vaccines might actually reach those people in hot countries whose lives depend on them. Another Duke way would be to seek to alter legislation affecting the status of migrant farmworkers in rural North Carolina. A way well-known to the Congregation at Duke Chapel would be to serve meals at the soup kitchen in Durham. But the relationship that brings about real change is friendship because to be a friend is to say, "I am allowing myself to be changed by knowing you." When we take stock of our relationship with the poor and oppressed during Lent, we ask ourselves, "Do I have friendships with people very different from myself, people to whom I say, 'I am allowing myself to be changed by knowing you'?"

Third, we reflect Mark's gospel by attending to Jesus' confrontation with the Jerusalem authorities of his day. We seem to have picked up an idea that holiness is a trancelike sense of peace and well-being in relation to all around you, an experience of floating on a magic carpet of tranquillity. Wherever that picture of holiness came from, it certainly wasn't Mark's gospel. Jesus is constantly having heated debates with everyone who held Israel in check. The one thing everyone seems to agree on today is that there's plenty wrong with the world. There are only two responses to this—either go and put it right yourself or, if you can't, make life pretty uncomfortable for those who can until they do. When we take stock of our relationship with the powerful this Lent, we ask ourselves, "Does the shape of my life reflect my longing to see God set people free, and do I challenge those who keep others in slavery?"

Just as for Mark's gospel, these three strands, the strands of accountable community, friendship with the poor, and challenge to the powerful, all unite in the fundamental story, which is our commissioning by God in our baptism, our sharing of the mystery of God in the transfiguration of our lives of service, and our entering the glory of God in our death and resurrection. But Mark's gospel teaches us that *this fundamental story cannot be lived except through the three strands of the story, except through accountable community, except through friendship with the poor, except through challenge to the powerful.* Of course, Christianity is about "my relationship with God," but there's no such thing as "my relationship with God" except as mediated through accountable community, friendship with the poor, and challenge to the powerful. Jesus' relationship with God was expressed, discovered, and revealed through accountable community, friendship with the poor, and challenge to the powerful. Why should ours be any different? Do we really think we have come up with a better way?

That brings us to the question of temptation. I know, I know. You've not been paying attention for the last ten minutes because your imagination has been captivated by the picture of Dean Wells as a little boy in short pants looking around furtively for his mother while his sticky hand ransacks the cookie jar. I guess that picture describes temptation because really it's stealing—the cookies really belong to the little boy's mother, and his greed makes him ignore that. But what about when the little boy grows up and the cookies really do belong to him? Surely it doesn't hurt anyone to have another cookie—even a chocolate one, with caramel just under the chocolate, and a little grated coconut on top? Somehow adulthood becomes a calculation of whether anyone gets hurt. Does it hurt anyone to drive a car fast on an empty road, to sleep with some of the best looking people in the Engineering School over the course of a few weekends, to blow a couple of hundred dollars on a pretty wild night in D.C., to rent an apartment that's way out of our income range? Once we've checked out that no one gets hurt and thus that it's none of anyone's business to pass comment, we're left alone in a sea that should be called desire but in fact is usually called anxiety because once capitalism has made greed a necessity and a virtue we're all anxious because we haven't got enough.

We think we're free with this new gospel of "it doesn't hurt anybody," but what we've done, if you look at it closely, is insulated ourselves from accountable community by making sure those around us can never criticize us. And we've insulated ourselves from friendship with the poor because we never count the poor into the equation when we're thinking about who does or doesn't get hurt. We seldom remember that the most common form of hurt is neglect, and we've insulated ourselves from making any challenge to the powerful because, by thoughtlessly joining our contemporary culture of acquisitiveness and gratification and rapid consumption, we are simply lining the pockets of those who make their money and keep their stranglehold on political influence by promoting that culture.

And then—wait for it, but don't condemn it too harshly, because we've all done it—then we have the extraordinary temerity to look at the big story—our baptism, our participation in the mystery of God, our future in God beyond death—and say we are a Christian, even though we have done next to nothing to reflect the ways Jesus mapped out the contours of what the life made possible by his ministry means. Temptation means trying to have the big story, trying to walk with God without the stories that make up the big story—

participation in an accountable community, friendship with the poor, and challenge to the powerful. Temptation is wanting to have all the benefits of Christian faith without any of the costs. Temptation is making God into a cookie jar. Temptation is trying to have God without Jesus.

But there's also another side of the coin. Getting any one of the strands out of proportion is also a temptation. Look at intimate community. We can easily fall into thinking that's all that matters. We can surround ourselves with people like us. We can spend our whole energy trying to make church or family a featherbed of insulated fuzziness, or we can even think intimacy is good in itself, that it doesn't much matter whom we are intimate with if our feelings are genuine and strong. This is the height of self-deception. When we make intimacy or community an end in itself, we fall into temptation.

It's the same in regard to friendship with the poor. At some stage, this must be harmonized with accountable community and challenge to the powerful. Discipleship isn't a lone quest, a wandering off into the ocean of need, a kind of cleansing by the fire of human pain. When we have discovered the depth of human need, we must not just give in to the temptation of anger or despair but gather a community of partners and confront those who maintain a pattern of oppression.

And again, in relation to challenging the powerful, while we must resist the temptation always to avoid conflict and be popular and say what people want to hear, we must not fall into thinking that there's always a simple explanation and the powerful are always to blame. We must not assume there's a theory that justifies our anger if such a theory tempts us to neglect our own friendship with the poor and commitment to accountable community.

All of these are temptations to have just a part of the gospel—just the community bit, just the poverty bit, or just the cage-rattling bit—without the rest. You could say they are temptations to remake Jesus in the image of our own needs and obsessions. These temptations take one of the three strands and ignore the big story. It is the temptation to have Jesus without God.

So, on the first Sunday in Lent, when we examine our Christian lives in the light of God's life and we examine our story in the light of Jesus' story, Mark's gospel leaves those of us who worship at

Duke Chapel with these three questions. Number one: Am I a disciple? That is, am I a member of a group of people, a religious life meeting, or some other fellowship that holds me to account and challenges me to put my life where my mouth is? Or do I surround myself with people who say things I want to hear? Number two: Am I a friend of the poor? Have I said to a single person, for whom life is a daily struggle and burden, "I am allowing myself to be changed by knowing you"? Am I spending time in that person's territory, taking seriously what God is doing in that person's life, and asking how I can help? Number three: Am I confronting oppression? Am I a thorn in the side of those who abuse and manipulate and extort and neglect? Or does the way I spend my money and the lifestyle I unthinkingly adopt simply underwrite and collude in patterns of exploitation and degradation?

We want to cut these strands of the story out. We want to cut out Mark's story and skip straight on to Easter. We want to cut straight to the cookie jar, but first we've got Lent. Time to look at ourselves in the mirror and ask hard questions. Am I really a disciple? Am I really a friend of the poor? Am I really confronting oppression? In other words, am I really following Jesus? We've got forty days to sort this out. Let's get on with it.

Following One Lord

This sermon was preached to the Duke Divinity School community in the divinity school's new Goodson Chapel, which sits beside Duke Chapel. The text is Matthew 16:13-19. I think of it more as a homily than as a sermon. The difference is that in a homily I am trying to make a pithy and satisfying exegetical insight or distinction and to offer enough illustration to convey the point clearly. In a sermon, I am seeking to offer a more comprehensive treatment that seeks at least in broad terms to place these observations in the light of the gospel as a whole, to reflect on issues raised, and to invite personal response. The key to a homily is its simplicity. This one was originally called "No Church without Jesus, No Jesus without Church," and its appeal lies in its constantly returning to its title as a statement not only of painful reality but also of good news.

Today we celebrate the confession of Peter. The word *confession* has two senses, and both of them apply here. Peter confesses the truth, and he confesses his sin. The *truth* that he confesses is that Jesus is the Messiah, the Son of the living God. The *sin* he confesses is that he, Peter, is too headstrong to imagine Jesus walking the way of the cross and too nervous to imagine going to the cross with him. I want to suggest to you that the first kind of confession, confessing faith, leads us to discover that there's no Jesus without the church, while the second kind of confession, confessing sin, leads us to discover that there's no church without Jesus.

So, first of all, no Jesus without church. How did Peter know that Jesus was both the Messiah, the fulfillment of all the hopes of Israel, and the Son of the living God, the subversion of all the claims of Rome? The answer is, because he'd been a disciple. He'd seen what the love of God in Jesus could do. He'd heard who God was and how God worked and what God had in store. He'd seen the transformation not only in his own life but also in the lives of friends and strangers. He'd seen that Jesus was everything God intended Israel to be and that in Jesus Israel had nothing to fear from Rome. Peter had learned who Jesus was by following him. He learned the way the church learns. There isn't any other way. No Jesus without church.

Who is it that tells us what Peter said? Matthew. The gospel writer. Or, as you've learned in your New Testament classes, the collection of sources with German names formerly known as Matthew. Who is Matthew, if not a person or a committee who lovingly recorded and shaped a whole host of stories about Jesus? Where did these stories come from? The church, of course. The earliest Christian communities. Who decided these stories as shaped by Matthew should be in the Bible? The church, of course. There is no Jesus except the Jesus disclosed to us by the early church. No Jesus without church.

How do we come to be reading Matthew today? How do we come to trust in this fragile document, handed down from papyrus to codicil to paper to scroll to tome to volume to leather-bound, zip-up, chain reference, study edition? What group has tried to follow Jesus and found its failures demonstrated as much as its successes? Who has for better or worse translated its own wisdom into the language of successive cultures and then found those cultures came back to criticize its life and its scripture without ever stopping to realize where its language for doing so came from? Who has carried the torch of such a tradition from one generation to another, through segregation, crusade, inquisition, and other things we might want to forget as well as acts of mercy, courageous marches, humble care of the young and the sick and the poor, and other things we too little remember? The church, of course. Without the church Jesus would be a forgotten word in today's world. No Jesus without church.

This is what we learn when we see that as soon as Peter declares that Jesus is the Christ, Jesus declares that on Peter will he found the church. The very moment when Jesus' identity is disclosed is the very moment when the church begins. Then, as now. The moment when we realize our life is all about Jesus, our community's life is all about Jesus, our neighborhood's life is all about Jesus, the world's life is all about Jesus, and that Jesus is all about God—this is the moment the church is born and continues to be born. No Jesus without church.

But "No Jesus without church" isn't all that we discover on the road to Caesarea Philippi. We know who Peter is. We know he is about to deny that the Messiah needs to go and suffer in Jerusalem. We know that when Jesus does go to Jerusalem Peter will scream that he will never betray Jesus and just as loudly a few hours later will scream when he realizes he's betrayed Jesus. We know who Peter is, and we know that Jesus knows who Peter is. So we understand what this means. It means the church will never be founded in such a way that it doesn't need rebuilding in every generation. It means it will never rest on the shoulders of one who doesn't have feet of clay. It means there will never be a leader who does not have to bend down and beg for forgiveness with tears in his or her eyes, and it means there will never be a church that doesn't fervently hope that its watching world will continue to look not on its fitful and faltering failures but on its transfigured and transforming Lord. It means no church without Jesus.

How I remember the day I stood in the bookstore with a pile of John Howard Yoder's books. I'd read a couple, and I'd decided this was the theologian who was going to change my life. Then a friend said, looking at the pile of books, "Did you know he's been in trouble for feeling up his female students?" And I wanted to know it

wasn't true, but it was true. And more. I knew people had muttered things at seminary about Barth and his secretary, and I knew
pretty much everyone in the seventies was talking about Tillich
and pretty well everyone, but somehow I wasn't quite so bothered
about Tillich. But not Yoder. Please not Yoder. For a while I didn't
want to read those books any more. I was just too hurt. But I did
read them, and what they taught me was No Church Without
Jesus. Then I looked again at Yoder's life, and I realized his life said
in a clumsier way than his books, No Church Without Jesus.

We'd all like to have perfect leaders, perfect theologians, perfect
disciples alongside us and around us and ahead of us. But in
founding his legacy on Peter, Jesus didn't give us perfection, he
gave us church. And church means facing up every day to the way
we've failed God, failed one another, and failed ourselves. Church
means entering every day into the cycle of repentance and confession and forgiveness and reconciliation and healing. Church means
walking every day the path of passion, cross, resurrection, and
exaltation. Church means getting up every day and saying, "Well,
you're not the pastor, the teacher, the friend, the spouse, the home
group leader, the vice chair of the stewardship and general purposes committee, the boss, the daughter, the son I thought I
wanted. You're not perfect, but then, I suppose, neither am I." This
isn't a perfection that doesn't need Jesus. This is church, which
needs Jesus every way every day. No Church without Jesus.

The Jesus we create without church is a fantasy. The church we
create without Jesus is a monster. Thank God that Peter knew who
Jesus was and that he found out the way the church finds out, by
following Jesus. And thank God that Jesus knew who Peter was
and founded the church on him anyway, so we can never fool ourselves that the church doesn't ever get beyond Jesus. No Church
without Jesus. No Jesus without Church. Thank God.

5

Speaking the Truth about Resurrection

In Three Tenses

This is an Easter sermon. Easter Sunday at Duke Chapel is overwhelming and unforgettable, with more than four thousand people attending the three services held that morning. This sermon followed Mark 16:1-8. Most Christians have a somewhat "blended" notion of the Easter story, so I find it helpful to change the text each year and explore dimensions of the story that would be missed if one were always to read Jesus and Mary in the garden from John's Gospel. As on Christmas Eve, there are many occasional churchgoers in the Chapel for a high feast day, and the sermon needs to be simple, direct, humorous, and memorable. The use of an accessible sermon structure enables me to introduce more challenging material under the radar without losing the congregation's concentration.

It's a very strange thing that thousands of us should gather in a university chapel to celebrate events that took place two millennia ago. It's strange because we live in a very different world from the world of our ancestors in the faith. For most of Christian history, people have been obsessed about two things that don't particularly bother us today. For starters, they were obsessed about the past. They took for granted that the most significant events in the world had already happened, that the Greek and Roman classical periods were the summit of human achievement in general, and that the manifestation of Jesus Christ in particular was the definitive moment in history. Alongside this, they were obsessed about the future. They knew that heaven and hell lasted forever, and they really didn't know which one they were going to, but there was nothing they cared about more, and they organized their lives and the whole of society around making sure they got to the right one.

Today we are different. We aren't obsessed with the past. We can't believe that people in the distant past knew better than we do. When things go wrong in international affairs, in government, or even on a college campus, we scratch our heads and think surely we've progressed beyond such mistakes and setbacks. We no longer see history as an incline heading downward from the classical era but as an incline heading upward with us at the highest point so far. And we aren't obsessed with the future. Democracy has become so much a part of our psyche that we assume everyone must go to heaven—it's in some vague sense part of every citizen's rights under the first amendment to the Constitution. Of course heaven is very much like here.

Today we are obsessed with the present. We no longer think of heaven as lost and gone and only partially to be recovered, or as far off and only dimly to be imagined. We think of heaven as a project to be realized, a commodity to be acquired the same way we acquire other commodities—by discovery, negotiation, or purchase. Moving into an empty house nine months ago from another country I rediscovered the commodities it seemed no sensible person could live without, and what each one represented. You need a telephone because it makes distant people present to you. You need television and the Internet because they make the world present to you—even the parts and the people you would never talk to on the telephone. You need a full medicine cabinet because it makes a hospital present in your own home. Piece by piece, you surround yourself with everything you need so that the past is present through photographs and mementos, and the uncertain future is managed through insurance policies and a sheaf of professional advisers. This obsession with the present is not just about old fuddy-duddies like me. The reason undergraduate life is so stressful is that the impulse to cram every possible ounce of experience into the present tense is physically and emotionally exhausting. However hard you read, study, play, party, make relationships, form ideas, you can't throw off the nagging anxiety that you're not cramming enough into this perpetual present tense and there's someone else who's cramming more in than you. If you think about it, every aspect of advertising is about persuading us that our lives are seriously deficient or even hopelessly inadequate without this new ingredient or experience or commodity becoming present to us.

This obsession with the present is, I think, why we find the question of God so problematic in our era. We work so hard to have life at our fingertips, with our TV and DVD remote controls, our cell phone, landline handset, iPod, and laptop all clustering on our sofa, that we are bewildered to find we can't have God at our fingertips. God remains elusive. God can't be turned into a commodity, just another way of bringing the mysterious past and the fearful future into the manageable present.

Of course all kinds of TV evangelists and self-help manuals do turn God into a gadget, a commodity that we can use as a bit of technology to acquire the goods we want. But we don't really trust such trite promises. Even so, we still struggle with the apparent absence of God in a world that values presence so highly. We struggle with the questions of suffering and evil because we demand that God be present to us in our times of confusion and despair. We struggle with the place of Christianity alongside other faiths because we can't see how God can be present there if he is supposed to be present here, and our democratic impulse says God must of course be evenly spread like some kind of divine peanut butter. We struggle with the proofs of God's existence because we want something knockdown and concrete that stops all this mysterious and elusive nonsense and brings God squarely into our manageable experience.

That brings us to Mark's account of the resurrection of Jesus Christ. This is the oldest Gospel account we have of the resurrection, but we seldom read it on Easter Day because we only see what is absent from it. There is no undisputable evidence of the resurrection. There is no straightforward account of what difference the resurrection makes to world history. There is no account of how the word got out to the male disciples, let alone the whole wide world, because it says the women remained silent. Worst of all, there is no account of an appearance of the risen Jesus. Small wonder that later editors added on to Mark's account the details we crave, details which in most Bibles appear in parentheses at the end of Mark's Gospel.

But I want to suggest to you that Mark's short account, these eight verses, gives us everything we need to know about the resurrection of Jesus. Not everything we *want* to know, of course, because we want to know a host of details that will bring this story into the present tense so we can turn it into a domestic gadget that will in the end replay to us nothing but an image of ourselves. Not everything we *want* to know about Jesus' resurrection, but everything we *need* to know.

The three faithful women come to the tomb early in the morning on the first day of the week, and they find the stone rolled away. They see a young man in a white robe, and he says three things to them. The first thing he says is about the past: "You are looking for Jesus of Nazareth, who was crucified. He has been raised; he is not here" (Mark 16:6). This is telling them everything they need to know about the past. He has been raised. Of course they have a host of questions: how can this be, was he really dead, is his risen body the same as his earthly body, does this mean we shall be raised in the same way, will he forgive those who put him to death, is there anything that is impossible with God? But there is only one question, it seems, they need to know the answer to: is this a physical resurrection or just a spiritual one? And the answer is, a physical one. The young man says, "He is not here. Look, there is the place they laid him" (Mark 16:6). So this is everything we need to know about the past: Jesus has been raised, not as a ghost or a spirit, a metaphor or an idea, but as a body.

The second thing the young man tells the women is about the present: "He is going ahead of you to Galilee" (Mark 16:7). This is telling them everything they need to know about the present. Jesus' resurrection is not a finished thing, a completed historical event with no further implications. Jesus is doing something now. He is going ahead. He is on the move. He is leading the action of God. He is setting an example, giving direction, defining purpose, pointing the way. And the place he is going is Galilee. It is not just that Jesus has opened the way into heaven, precious as that news would be; it is that he has opened the way back to a new life on earth, and in Galilee, the place the disciples knew best, their home, the place where they had lived all their lives before Jesus summoned them to the way of the cross. The news about the past told the women that Jesus had changed everything they took for granted about cause and effect, the disaster of the cross, and the tragedy of their own failure. Now the news about the present told them that Jesus was effecting that change in their very homes and habitat, among those they knew best and around those who lived far from the dramatic stage of Jerusalem. This is everything we need to know about the present: Jesus is on the move.

The third thing the young man tells the women is about the future: "There you will see him"(Mark 16:7). The young man tells the women everything they need to know about the future. Jesus' resurrection changes not just the things you thought you knew about reality, including the places and the people you thought you knew best; Jesus' resurrection is going to transform *you*. You will see him. You are going to find yourself in Jesus' presence. You are going to be his companion. This is the destiny of your life. And there isn't any other news. This is the last word. So we have to assume "there you will see him" really is all we need to know about the future. We shall be in Jesus' company, presumably forever.

You have to admire Mark's economy of style here. Surely he knew more than he is telling us—at the very least, the women must have told someone, or the story would never have reached Mark. But Mark doesn't tell us everything he knows. He just tells us everything we need to know. He doesn't tell us enough to make the resurrection of Jesus just another remote control on our sofa, just another device for giving us the world at our fingertips and bringing all human experience into our living room. We can't domesticate Mark's Gospel. We'd love to have the explicit details, the biology, physics and chemistry of resurrection, the physical evidence, and the full interactive DVD color package. Mark withholds all this. But look what he does tell us. He does tell us the vital information about the past—Jesus is risen; the vital information about the future—we shall see him; and the vital information about the present—we are on our way from the place of resurrection to the gate of glory.

What more do we need? These eight short verses give us a pretty comprehensive summary. They give us the gospel—Christ is risen; they give us our hope—we shall see him; and they give us our mission—he is going ahead of you. That's Easter. That's the Christian faith. Hallelujah. Everything we need to know about the past, everything we need to know about the present, and everything we need to know about the future. I think that's more than enough, don't you?

In One Week

This is a sermon on the text John 20:19-31, originally entitled "What Does the Resurrection Really Mean?" The passage is usually assumed to be about Thomas, and sermons on this text are conventionally about persisting amid doubts. I intended two things in this sermon. One was to address the question of why and how John ends his Gospel and to point to the significance of the closing words of John 20. The second was to take a serious intellectual analysis of barriers to faith and to see that this passage has a great deal to say about those barriers. In that sense, it is a combination of an exegetical sermon, expounding the text, and a theological sermon, exploring the issues raised. It was delivered on Reunion Weekend. Rather than offer alumni/ae stories of great deeds done then or now, I chose to demonstrate that an intelligent exploration of Christian faith in all its joy and complexity is alive and well at their beloved Duke Chapel.

Christians believe God is all love and all power. That's why the heart of God breaks when Jesus hangs on the cross: because the overwhelming love of God that adores humankind is in unbearable tension with the overwhelming power of God that longs to obliterate evil. God's heart is all love and all power, and we see them both on Good Friday. On Good Friday, God's heart breaks when his love and his power are going in opposite directions.

There are two main reasons why people stop believing in God. They either stop believing that God is all love or they stop believing that God is all power. We could call the first reason the moral reason. Its most famous exponent is Ivan Karamazov, in Dostoyevsky's novel *The Brothers Karamazov.* Ivan tells the story of a vindictive farmer who punishes a wayward child by tying him to a cart and having a horse drag the cart all round the farm, leading to the child's grisly death. Ivan angrily shouts that if there is a God who has a heaven ready for us, and if that God allows suffering like the suffering of that child, then that heaven isn't worth going to. In Ivan's words, "I . . . most respectfully return him the ticket."[1] The moral rejection of God doesn't question the existence or power of God; it just questions the goodness of God.

The second reason for stopping believing in God we could call the philosophical reason. Its most explicit exponent is Woody Allen. You'll remember his famous words, "If it turns out that there is a God, then basically he's an underachiever." This is a rejection of the belief that God is all power. Now this can come in a variety of forms. Some people carry on believing in an all-powerful force but stop believing that that force is also all-loving. For example, Marxists believe in this way in class conflict and the emergence of the proletariat, and extreme Darwinists believe in this way in natural selection and the capacity of species to imitate and adapt. Other people continue to hold some kind of a belief in the divine quality of love but cease to believe that that divine love is all-powerful. For example, one congregation was appalled when a nightclub opened up next door to the church building. Questions about the well-being of the nightclub began to make veiled appearances in the regular intercessions; hostility was being dressed up as piety. One night the nightclub burned down. The nightclub owner wanted to prosecute the church, for he was aware that many members had prayed for just such a turn of events. But the congregation denied any involvement and seemed as surprised as everyone else. Like a lot of churches, that church assumed God was all-loving but had long ago stopped believing that God was all-powerful.

Today's Gospel reading concludes with one of the most baffling statements in all of scripture: "Now Jesus did many other signs in the presence of his disciples, which are not written in this book" (John 20:30). I beg your pardon. You mean to say, Mr. John, or shall I be formal and call you the Fourth Evangelist, you mean to say that you know a whole lot more about Jesus that you're not telling us? You cannot be serious! How tantalizing is that? You've convinced us that Jesus is the central character in world history and then you say, "That's all, folks! Story time is over. Time for bed."

It's not surprising that we drool over reports of new Gospels found, new archaeological discoveries made, new insights into the life and character of Jesus. When we have come to love someone, let alone depend on him for our eternal destiny, we want to know every last detail about him. We don't want to be informed, "That's all I'm going to say."

Yet John goes on to tell us, "But these are written so that you may come to believe that Jesus is the Messiah, the Son of God, and that through believing you may have life in his name" (John 20:31). I want to look closely at this sentence: "So that you may come to believe that Jesus is the *Messiah*, the *Son of God*." I want to suggest to you that John's concern in summarizing his Gospel is precisely to address the two questions I have just been exploring. Is God all love? And is God all power?

Let's start with the first question, the moral question. Is God good? The way John answers this question is to assert that Jesus is the Messiah. Why is it so important to John that we believe that Jesus is the Messiah? Well, principally because John wants us to know that we can trust God. John tells us that Jesus is the Messiah in order to assure us that God is good. God keeps his promises.

This means first of all that God keeps his promises to Israel. The Old Testament is a litany of God's promises to his chosen people. John's Gospel is the story of how all these promises find their yes in Christ. Jesus is the new Moses, who gives his people bread in the wilderness. Jesus is the new Elijah, who raises a beloved man from death. Jesus is the new Isaiah, who speaks for God's people in exile and becomes the suffering servant who takes away the people's sins. Jesus is the new Jeremiah, who meets God's people in a time of desperation and scarcity and gives them joy and abundance, bringing home all the outcasts and the excluded to his wondrous kingdom. Jesus is the new Ezekiel, offering in his own body the new Temple that reconciles God and his people. And God does to Jesus one thing he never once did to any of the prophets: he raises Jesus to new life. Jesus is the Messiah.

John doesn't just show us how the resurrected Jesus fulfills the promises God made in the Old Testament. He also shows us how Jesus keeps the promises he himself made earlier in the Gospel. There are at least four such fulfillments in today's reading. The first time John the Baptist speaks about Jesus in John 1, he says, "Among you stands one whom you do not know, the one who is coming after me" (John 1:26-27). Here, when Jesus appears to the disciples in John 20, we have the very same words: "Jesus came and stood among them" (John 20:19). The first thing that happens to Jesus in John 1 is that he receives the Holy Spirit in being baptized by John. The first thing that happens to the disciples when Jesus appears to them in John 20 is that they receive the Holy Spirit as Jesus breathes upon them. There are also two promises Jesus fulfills from his last words to the disciples before his betrayal and death. In John 14:27, Jesus says, "Peace I leave with you; my peace I give to you. I do not give to you as the world gives." Here in John 20:19, sure enough, Jesus' first words are, "Peace be with you." Then in John 16:22 Jesus promises, "I will see you again, and your hearts will rejoice, and no one will take your joy from you." And sure enough, here in John 20:20, the first thing John tells us after Jesus has finished speaking is, "Then the disciples rejoiced when they saw the Lord."

These are all ways in which John is telling us that Jesus is the Messiah. Jesus is the one promised by God, and God keeps his promises, and Jesus fulfilled God's promises and made promises of his own, and in the resurrection he kept those promises too. God is good. You can trust him.

So let's turn to the second question, the philosophical question. Is God powerful? The way John answers this question is to say Jesus is the Son of God. Why does this title matter so much? Why, when it comes to summarizing his Gospel in a single sentence, does John choose the title Son of God alongside Messiah to identify Jesus? Well, because there was one man in the ancient world who habitually assigned to himself this title, a man who ruled the known world and had the power of life and death over pretty much every living thing that moved or breathed on the face of the earth. And that man was the Roman Emperor. The Roman Emperor called himself the Son of God. So when we read in Mark's and Matthew's Gospels that when Jesus breathed his last on the cross and the centurion said, "Truly this man was the Son of God," we're not talking about a centurion who carefully did the sums in his head—"darkness, drama, agonizing suffering, true goodness—it all adds up to something special: only one way to describe him—the Son of God." No, it's far more significant than that. The centurion, the man who put Jesus to death, stands at the foot of the cross, sees a dying man, and proclaims, "This dying man is my true Emperor, and I shall be loyal to him even if it costs me my loyalty to the so-called Emperor in Rome. *This* man, not the Emperor, is the real Son of God." It's a sensational statement for a Roman commander to make. We get a similar statement from Thomas in today's Gospel. After Jesus has fulfilled all the promises of God in appearing to the disciples on the first day of the week, proving himself to be the Messiah, he comes back a week later and appears again, this time with Thomas present, and what does Thomas say? What does Thomas say? "My Lord and my God"—in Latin, *Dominus deusque*—another title given to the Roman Emperor. So the disciples on Easter Day greet Jesus as the Messiah, and Thomas a week later greets Jesus as the Son of God. The disciples recognize that Jesus is the God of the Jews, and Thomas recognizes that Jesus is the God of the whole world too. What Thomas sees is something the Roman Emperor could never aspire to, something beyond the imagination of even the most powerful force on earth: what Thomas sees is power over death. Jesus stands before him, having died on the cross just ten days earlier. This is power, awesome, astonishing, glorious power, and power in the hands of one who continues to be gracious, loving, and forgiving even after his disciples' betrayal, denial, and desertion.

So we begin to see why John feels there is little left to say. He has shown us that the God of Israel is faithful, keeps his promises, and fulfills his scripture. God is good. And John has shown us that the God of the whole world puts Roman might to shame and overcomes even the horror of death. God is powerful. John demonstrates how God meets our doubts and skepticism at every turn. God is good, and God is powerful. John's story has given us the whole gospel in his account of Jesus' resurrection. There is only one thing more to hope for, the one part of John's sentence we haven't yet talked about: "But these are written so that you may come to believe that Jesus is the Messiah, the Son of God, and that through believing *you may have life in his name.*"

There is actually a third reason why people don't believe in God. It's not a moral or philosophical one. It's simply that they don't get around to it. God is all-loving and all-powerful, but they've got other things on their minds. A while ago I saw a story in a London newspaper. The story began by saying that there was a wealthy landowner in Ireland. The old landowner died leaving a huge fortune. When his attorneys found his last will and testament, they discovered he had only one heir. That heir was nowhere to be found. They issued invitations on the radio and in newspapers, but there was no response. Twenty years later, after a man died in a night shelter in London, he was discovered to have been the missing heir. He never knew about the enormous fortune, let alone claimed it, because he had never gotten around to being in touch with his Irish cousins.

How many of us are like that man? Wandering alone in misery and despair, even though there is news of breathtaking joy, but we have never gotten around to believing it. The pathos in the story of the man in the night shelter we should feel for ourselves. The difference is, we can do something about it. John's Gospel is a great gift to us. It shows us on the one hand that God is all-loving, that he forgives even after the cross, that he is faithful, that we can trust him. It shows us on the other hand that God is all-powerful, that there is no human power that can compare to him, and that he can overcome even the power of death. God is all love, and God is all power. The gift of John's Gospel is that, through meeting Jesus in it, we may find resurrection life, a life suffused with forgiveness and love, a life free from the fear of oppression and death. But to find that life we must believe the gospel of Jesus. We must claim the inheritance, embody the love, receive the power. And through believing, we will have life in his name.

In Four Words

This sermon, on John 11:1-44 (although not all the verses were read aloud), is the kind of sermon I most enjoy preaching because it is the kind of sermon I most enjoy hearing. I sometimes say I have two sermons: the one that says, "These may look like a few Bible verses, but, in fact, they are God's story of everything," and the one that says, "This looks like a tricky issue, but let's bring the full theological resources of the tradition to bear on it." This sermon is squarely of the former kind. The key decision to make in preaching a sermon like this is whether one expects the congregation to be following the scriptural verses as one is speaking. While there are Bibles at every seat in Duke Chapel, this is not the tradition in which most of the congregation has been shaped, and so I offer here a way of preaching an exegetical sermon without assuming that the congregation is following every scriptural word. The sermon was preached at All Saints, and I include references to the season toward the end, but for me the need to explain and enjoy the festival was less important than the opportunity to lay out one of the most dazzling narratives in the New Testament. Being a long passage, it needs to be made accessible to the congregation, and I chose my familiar pattern of perceiving a series of thresholds in the account. The rhetorical approach is to overwhelm the congregation with wave upon wave of good news, with the result that listeners are left thrilled and eager to explore for themselves.

Every morning on ESPN there is a countdown of the top ten plays of the previous day's sporting contests. We see the best touchdown, the best basket, the best home run. Every now and again, we see a move that has everything that sport has to offer— speed, skill, teamwork, surprise, and success. I want to suggest to you that if on the last day the heavenly equivalent of ESPN put together its top ten moments in salvation history, the raising of Lazarus would be up there—because it has everything.

The Gospel of John locates itself at the center of time. Its prologue harkens back to the creation itself, with the words, "In the beginning." Jesus' incarnation as the Word made flesh is the fulfillment of the logic of creation, in which the Word made the world. By concluding with Jesus' resurrection, John's Gospel anticipates the end of time, the final moment of resurrection for all that God transforms to be in the presence of the Trinity forever. So in twenty-one chapters, John's Gospel gives us a miniversion of everything from the beginning of time to the end.

The raising of Lazarus comes in John 11, the central chapter out of the twenty-one chapters. This story is right at the center of time, and it tells the story of how Jesus crosses three thresholds to bring about resurrection. At the beginning of the story, verse 7 tells us, Jesus is outside Judaea. There is much talk about why Jesus takes so long to come to Lazarus's aid. Think about what this might mean in the context of the whole gospel, of salvation history. Jesus crossing into Judaea is like Jesus coming to earth and becoming incarnate. In both cases there is a strange delay. Why didn't God come among us in Jesus the first time anything went wrong? Listen to these words from verse 4 as we contemplate the many situations of suffering and sadness in our world today: "This illness does not lead to death; rather, it is for God's glory, so that the Son of God may be glorified through it." Jesus crosses the threshold into Judaea, he comes into the life of the world, and as his disciples point out in verse 8, the Judaeans, that's to say the Jerusalem authorities, are out to get him.

The second threshold Jesus crosses in verse 17 is that he comes to Bethany. We can see a close correspondence between the role of Bethany in this story and the role of Israel in the whole story of the gospel. Why doesn't Jesus come to the whole world? Because he's a real human being who can only be in one place at a time. Why does he come to Israel, why does he come to Martha and Mary, rather than any other nation or people? Because God loves Israel, just as we're told in verse 5 that Jesus loved Martha and her sister and Lazarus. What does Jesus do in Bethany; in other words, what does he do in Israel? He meets people's needs, and he speaks the truth. As verse 30 reminds us, Jesus spent most of his time on the outskirts of the village—and on the outskirts of Israel. He had disclosed his purpose before he came to earth and before he came to the center of Israel by his proclamation in the Old Testament and his proclamation and ministry in Galilee.

The third threshold Jesus crosses is in verse 38 when he comes to the tomb. Here we can see the correspondence between the place of the tomb in this story and the place of Jerusalem in the gospel story. It's the place of horror and the place of transformation. It's the place of impurity and yet the place where, Jesus says in verses 4 and 40, we shall see the glory of God. At this point we realize that Jesus has performed six miracles prior to this central moment in John's Gospel. He turned water into wine, he healed the official's son in Cana, he healed the man at the pool of Bethzatha, he fed the five thousand, he walked on water, and he healed the man born blind. We're about to witness the perfect seven.

This story tells us everything about the Gospel of John and everything about how the Gospel of John fits into the whole story of God. But that's not all it tells us. It shows us everything about Jesus. First of all it tells us he's fully human. He loves Lazarus, and he loves Martha and Mary. He loves them so much, and he finds the chaos of opposition and grief and misunderstanding and responsibility and power so overwhelming that in verse 33 his whole body is convulsed with passion. The words in this translation don't do it justice by saying he was disturbed and deeply moved. It's better to say he shuddered and was transfixed; this was a whole body experience. It's telling us that there was nothing in Jesus' body, mind, or spirit that was not overcome by the intensity of this moment. Again, it reinforces that this is the center of the gospel story. And then in verse 35 we have one of the most famous verses in Scripture, perhaps because it's one of the shortest: "Jesus wept" (KJV). Why did he weep? Well, of course because he loved Lazarus. But don't miss the irony of the words that immediately precede this verse. In John 1:39 the words "Come and see" are the way Jesus invites his first followers into the journey of discipleship. "Come and see" becomes the clarion call to follow Jesus. And here in verse 34, these very words are said *to* Jesus, and they are a reminder to him and to us that discipleship leads to the tomb.

So this story shows us that Jesus is fully human, but it also shows us that Jesus is fully divine. What the story takes for granted is that no one—you, me, or anyone in the modern or ancient world—has ever seen anything like this, a man in the tomb for four days, bound in the clothes of death, walking out of that tomb alive. Only God can do this. But the divinity doesn't just lie in the miracle. The human drama of this story, with all its emotion and surprise and horror and glory, is in some ways only a backdrop to the drama of Jesus' relationship with his Father. In spite of the grief, in spite of the stench, in spite of the hostility, in spite of the horror, Jesus insists in verse 40 that this story in its beginning and ending is always a story about God: "Did I not tell you that if you believed, you would see the glory of God?" When you consider Jesus' shuddering and being convulsed in the light of his relationship with his Father, you can see that these profound physical and emotional reactions are not just the essence of his humanity but the essence of his divinity. He is bearing in his body the full weight of his relationship with the Father. This is in anticipation of the cross, and, like the cross, it prefigures the resurrection. So when Jesus speaks directly to the Father in verses 41 and 42, his words are words almost of relief: "Father, I thank you for having heard me. I knew that you always hear me, but I have said this for the sake of the crowd standing here, so that they may believe that you sent me." They remind us of Jesus' last words on the cross, "It is finished," and they anticipate John's last words in chapter 20, where he says that the gospel has been written "so that you may come to believe."

So this story tells us everything about John's Gospel and everything about Jesus. But there's more. It tells us everything about life and death. If John 11 is the center of John's Gospel, then Jesus' conversation with Martha in verses 21 to 27 is the center of the center. Martha says to Jesus, "I know that [Lazarus] will rise again in the resurrection on the last day," and Jesus says to her, "I am the resurrection and the life. Those who believe in me, even though they die, will live, and everyone who lives and believes in me will never die. Do you believe this?" Martha responds, "Yes, Lord, I believe that you are the Messiah, the Son of God, the one coming into the world." The resurrection *and* the life. When Jesus says, "I am the resurrection," he is saying, "I am the *power* of God overcoming evil and death." When Jesus says, "I am the life," he is saying, "I am the *love* of God making possible new relationships, new communities, new possibilities for human flourishing and worship and joy." You've heard it from me before and you'll hear it again: the American church is divided between those who think it's all about power and those who think it's all about love. Some want to read just "I am the resurrection" and stick to believing the right things and concentrating on eternal salvation, and others want to read just "I am the life" and major in creating a just society and sticking with issues in this present world. But Jesus says, "I am the resurrection *and* the life"—I am about doctrine *and* justice, about this world *and* the next, about the individual *and* about community and society, about power *and* love.

Finally, this story tells us everything about discipleship. The story is a training manual in what it means to be a saint. The disciple prays to God in an attitude of need and expectation. Is this the way you pray? Need and expectation. Mary and Martha express need in the words in verse 3, "Lord, he whom you love is ill," and they express expectation in the words in verse 22, "But even now I know that God will give you whatever you ask of him." As disciples of Jesus today, we stand before him in need and expectation. Saints don't expect that they and those they love will never suffer, will never be bewildered or disappointed, but they do expect that if they believe, they will see the glory of God. They empty their hearts of the self-deception that prevents them from expressing their need, and they empty their lives of the inhibition that prevents them from articulating their expectation. The more we are around Jesus, the more we become aware of our need of him and the more reason we have to expect that he will transform us and the whole of reality. We also discover in this story that discipleship involves danger. In verse 8, the disciples recall that Jesus' enemies tried to stone him the last time he went to Judaea. In verse 16, Thomas faces up to the reality more than any other disciple in the Gospel and says, "Let us also go, that we may die with him." Being a saint means dying with Jesus.

We discover that discipleship means being with Jesus in the face of disgust and fear. Jesus says in verse 39, "Take away the stone." Martha protests that surely this has gotten beyond a joke. You may be the resurrection and the life and all that, but you're not going to expose us to that kind of stench? You cannot be serious! Jesus says, in as many words, "Are you going to let your bourgeois sense of propriety stop you from seeing the glory of God?" (Not a bad question for us to ask ourselves as we read this story today.) Saints discover that the most important work of God seems to happen in places where the smell is pretty bad.

There are a couple more things this story shows us about discipleship. In Martha we see that discipleship involves expressing faith in Jesus. It's not clear whether the story would have continued had Martha not made her response of faith to Jesus in verse 27. What's more transparent is that those who don't believe don't get to see the glory of God. They may see the stunt, they may see the drama, but they don't get to see the glory.

At the end of the story, we see how disciples are to respond to the miracle that Christ performs. This is the way God makes us into saints. Remember at the end of the feeding of the five thousand the disciples' job was to make sure everyone got enough and to clear up afterward and ensure that nothing was wasted? Well here it's similar. The instructions in verse 44 are "Unbind him and let him go." When you learn Greek in seminary, the first word you learn is *luo*—which means "I loose." You think you're learning it because it's the simplest verb, but one day you find your way to the end of the central story in the story that is itself the story at the center of the world. At the end of this story you find this word with which you began your studies, and you find it doesn't just mean *loose*; it means *unbind*. And it doesn't just mean *unbind*; it means *set free*. And it doesn't just mean *set free*; it means *forgive*. And it doesn't just mean *forgive*; it means *be a participant in resurrection*. It means the whole gospel.

So now you see why I said at the beginning that the raising of Lazarus is one of those stories they play over and over again in heaven because it's a highlights package of salvation history and it's at the center of the gospel. It tells us everything about the Gospel of John. It shows us everything about Jesus. It demonstrates everything about life and death. It portrays everything about discipleship. In fact, there's only one question that really matters that it doesn't answer for us. It gives us a suggested answer in the mouth of Martha, but the one thing it can't do is answer the question for us. It gives us the gospel, it offers us Jesus, it holds out to us resurrection life, and it describes what it means to respond. It leaves us with one remaining question: "Do you believe this?"

In Two Words

This Easter Day sermon, on Matthew 28:1-10, has the structure of a homily but the scope of a sermon. Its delight is intended to lie in its simplicity. The whole sermon builds up to the last line, which I delivered three times—first in a whisper, again with hands cupped, and finally with an expression of explicit but still understated joy. When one has a captivating ending like this, all one needs to do is to structure the sermon so that the congregation is in exactly the right place to hear the final words. (I try not to commit a single word to paper until I have worked out what the final line will be; it is a good discipline.) Being such a festive occasion, Easter is a good moment to consider the greatest questions about human and cosmic life—and to point out that these were exactly the questions in the Gospel writers' minds as they gave us these precious accounts. Simplicity is not always a virtue in preaching, but the secret of a major festival sermon is to crystallize the gospel in one exhilarating moment.

Today is a day of emotions so powerful you can smell them, like the bouquet of spices in a Middle Eastern bazaar. Easter. The nerve center of the Christian faith. The biggest day in world history. The day death died. The shape of the church's creed blended together with the rhythm of the season so that Christ's bursting from the tomb is echoed in a myriad of budding flowers and blossoming trees. Truth, beauty, goodness—today they have the upper hand. Through crucifixion tears, we sense a hint of resurrection glory. Can it be true?

Of all the feelings and passions of Easter, I want to focus our hearts on two—two emotions that embody the energy of today. I want to take you back to that distant Sunday morning, the first day of the week, when the dew lay heavy, the sun was warming up, the birds were shaking sleep away with the thrill of dawn, and all creation breathed in the smell of anticipation. Two people rose early, their sandaled feet covered in dust and strained by running. They went to the tomb and met there an angel who broke open their whole world by saying, "He is not here; for he has been raised" (Matthew 28:6). Feel the intensity of their emotion; smell it. Saint Matthew tells us what they did and what they felt. They ran. They ran, with fear and great joy. With fear and great joy. And we can see them running, with fear, with the hasty, gulping breath of fear, and with gurgling joy, with the outstretched hands and billowing cloak and squealing yelps of joy.

Fear and great joy: at the heart of the resurrection and at the heart of the Bible. Fear of judgment: Adam and Eve, banished from the garden; Cain, discovered to be a murderer; David, exposed as a scheming adulterer; Israel itself, thrown into exile as a result of its sin. Fear of holiness: of the God Moses met in the burning bush and met again on Mount Sinai amid thunder, lightning, fire, and smoldering cloud. Fear of the coming day of the Lord, the day when God "will utterly sweep away everything from the face of the earth" (Zephaniah 1:2). Fear to take any risk, like the third servant in the talent parable who buried his talent in the ground. Terrible fear.

And yet also great joy. After forty days of rain and one hundred fifty days of flood, Noah sends out the dove, and it returns with an olive branch. After the shame of the tower of Babel, God calls Abraham to be the father of a nation. As the ark of the covenant is brought into Jerusalem, David dances before the Lord. As Ezra reads out the books of the Law to the returning exiles, they weep with joy. As Elizabeth greets Jesus' mother-to-be, Elizabeth feels the babe within her own womb leap for joy. Zacchaeus picks up his skirts and runs home with glee to prepare a kingdom banquet for Jesus. The father of the prodigal son is bursting with joy to see his wayward son come home. Great, great joy.

Fear and great joy: at the heart of the resurrection and at the heart of the experience of faith today. Fear that some new discovery will discredit the historic faith of the church. "Archaeologists find Jesus' laptop," screams one headline. Turns out, Jesus' DVD collection included some Handel, a good deal of Mahler, and the full set of Peter, Paul, and Mary. Fear that the fabric of the society that has shaped the gospel will come apart, that marriage and family life are disintegrating, that major denominations are mired in self-doubt, that other faiths and new technologies will dismantle any sense of certainty we may still have. Fear that we're just not good enough to be a Christian, that Jesus calls us to peace when we know our own violence, that Jesus calls us to generosity when we know our own selfishness, that Jesus calls us to the way of the cross when we know we're terrified to die. Horrifying fear.

And yet also great joy. Joy when you discover that love isn't just a slushy word or a passing feeling but that it became flesh in Jesus Christ. Joy when, after years of living under the burden of guilt and self-hatred for something you've done, you finally hear the words, "You are forgiven" and know it's true. Joy when all your anger and frustration and despair about suffering and cruelty and hatred in the world are transcended when you hear a voice saying, "This is what you are to do," and you realize that it's your vocation and you have a part to play in God's story after all. Joy when you're going through a hard time and someone from your church leaves a card or brings some food or gives you a look that says, "I don't know you very well, but we're both part of the body of Christ, so I'm here for you." Joy when you meet a person very different from you, a person whose face or manner or language you find a little alarming, but in whom you come to discover you've met Christ. Joy when a person says to you, "I don't know if it's something you said, or just doing some of this stuff with you, but I've come to believe in Jesus, and my life has been transformed." Joy. Fabulous joy.

Fear and great joy: at the heart of the resurrection and at the extremes of our hearts today. So much to fear, so many reasons to be afraid. Fear for ourselves, that we'll experience crushing disappointment, that our faith will turn to dust, that our hopes will be illusions and our critical friends be proved correct. Fear for those we love. Fear that however much we love and however much we care, we shall still have to face the awful moment of parting, of letting go, of aching loss and separation. Fear that we can't protect our loved ones from the horror of death. And fear about issues way beyond our control, from terrorism and war that destroy countries to the addictions and diseases that destroy lives to the greed and plunder that are destroying the earth. So much to fear.

And yet also great joy. Great joy. Joy of a baa-lamb finding its rickety feet in a meadow; joy of a baby discovering how to swallow; joy of the song when we have the words and God has the tune; joy of the harvest when all is fresh and mellow. The joy of friendship, of those we have known and loved through thick and thin. The joy of forgiveness, when bitterness and failure do not get the last word. The joy of creation, when we hear birds chirrup on a spring morning. The joy of being part of a team, when you believe in what you are doing and where you are going. The joy of the orchestra, about to break into a thrilling crescendo. The joy of a craftsman, perfecting his wood. The joy of today is feeling all our love, and the love for us, that is in the world and then realizing that that intensity, that love, is just a keyhole we look through, and beyond is a shimmering garden of delight. Just a keyhole, and we look together on God's garden, restored and glorious. Great joy. Great, great joy.

So here we are, at the moment when the angel's words break open our lives, and we start to run with fear and great joy. Fear and joy, the two poles, the two extremes of our human response to the awesome intimacy of God. Fear and joy run with us throughout our lives together, as constant reminders of the cost and promise of following Jesus. Fear and joy, at the center of our longings, at the heart of our desires.

But there is a secret. It is a secret that we can only glimpse at in this life. It is a secret that was first revealed to those two early risers on the first day of the week, while all creation breathed in the aroma of anticipation. It is the secret of Easter. It is a secret that I pray we will realize in the course of the year to come. It is a secret that is the climax of our gospel, a secret of the mystery of fear and joy. And the secret is this: joy wins.

Notes

1. Fyodor Dostoyevsky, *The Brothers Karamazov*, trans. Richard Pevear and Larissa Volokhonsky (New York: Vintage Books, 1991), 245.

6

Speaking the Truth about Salvation

Heaven

This sermon and the one that follows were preached on successive Sundays of Advent. They provoked so much discussion that I set up a special discussion session to give people a chance to converse about these ideas. About half of this sermon is given over to clearing away dead wood. I seldom use this technique because it invariably results in the congregation's remembering more of what the preacher was against than about what the preacher was commending. However, the dead wood addressed in the first half of this sermon is so pervasive that it badly needs to be named for what it is. Part of the constructive power of this sermon was that those who had heard many of my sermons had grown used to hearing the words *worship* and *friendship*, but here there is a more thoroughgoing attempt to show why such words are so important. The truth is that what people most deeply heard was the critical material in the first half of the sermon. Wherever such half-baked notions of the afterlife come from, they die hard.

On the four Sundays of Advent it was once the tradition for the preacher to address the Four Last Things—death, judgment, heaven, and hell—or what are known at Duke as the Final Four. It's easy to see why this tradition has been discontinued in a university setting. The problem is that the undergraduates all disappear after the second week with a pretty good understanding of death and judgment but never having heard of heaven. All pain and no gain. So today I'm going to cut to the chase and talk about heaven.

Two obsessions have prevented preachers from talking much about heaven over the years. The first obsession, which you'll recognize, is what revivalist preaching is largely about. It's the harrowing anxiety about who gets into heaven and who gets sent to hell and the determination to do whatever it takes to make sure one is in the group going upstairs rather than downstairs. The more significant question of what heaven is like for those who get there never seems to come up in these discussions.

The second obsession is a much more contemporary one. It's about offering words of comfort to the bereaved. Setting aside the conventional language of heaven and hell leaves us as a culture with a desperate search for platitudes in the face of the agony of losing a friend or relative. Pastors avoid facing hard theological and philosophical questions in the mistaken notion that their principal role is to offer comfort, however superficial and clichéd that comfort may be. But the truth is that you can't enjoy the glory of heaven without first facing the reality of death.

What I'd like to do is to describe three things heaven is not before going on to describe three things heaven is. In between, I'd like to suggest a way we might distinguish between the truth of heaven and what we might regard as second-rate imitations. I understand that sometimes grief is so profound that we can cast off from our theological moorings in search of comfort, but my aim today is to show that what the Bible promises us about heaven is so much greater than what is on offer from Hallmark greetings cards.

So, here goes with three things heaven is not. Heaven is not the continuation of a person's eternal soul. Countless people over the centuries have taken comfort in the belief that, while their loved one's body lies moldering in the grave, his or her soul goes marching on. I'm sorry to tell you, but this isn't a belief rooted in Christian theology. The dualist idea that we are essentially physical bodies and spiritual souls, which become detached at death whereupon we continue simply as spiritual souls—this idea is one that arises among the Greek philosophers centuries before Christ. It's not something the Old Testament comprehends. For the Bible, humans are one in life, body and soul; and one in death, body and soul. Death is real. When Canon Henry Scott Holland said in Saint Paul's Cathedral on Whitsunday 1910 the words, "Death is nothing at all. I have only slipped away into the next room. . . . Life . . . is the same as it ever was. There is absolutely unbroken continuity," he was certainly offering words of comfort, but he wasn't preaching orthodox Christian theology. Can anyone look at Jesus on the cross and say, "Death is nothing at all"? Can anyone look at the aftermath of a suicide bombing in a market square and imagine the words, "I have only slipped away into the next room"? Our death is the end of us. Our hope lies not in pretending otherwise but in knowing that our death is not the end of God.

Here's the second thing heaven is not. Heaven is not our reabsorption into the infinite. This idea that when we die we blend back into the ground of being is a mixture of the simply biological assumption that we dissolve into the soil and the quaintly spiritual notion that we become part of the ether. Just as the champion of the eternal soul argument is Henry Scott Holland, so the great exemplar of the reabsorption argument is Mary Frye. I'm sure you'll know the lines,

> I am a thousand winds that blow.
> I am the diamond glints on snow.
> I am the sunlight on ripened grain.
> I am the gentle autumn rain.[1]

Again, these are comforting words, but they seem to have come out of a worldview that has stopped caring whether a belief is true as long as it's comforting. Note that, like the Scott Holland piece, God is wholly absent from this understanding of heaven. Jesus seems to have achieved nothing of any significance in his cross and resurrection, at least as far as our death and life thereafter are concerned. Perhaps the reason that the verses usually entitled "Death is nothing at all" and "Do not stand by my grave and weep" have become so enormously popular in our contemporary culture is that they offer pictures of continuity beyond death that require no belief in God or reference to Jesus whatsoever. The trouble is, they do so by denying the reality of death, and the pictures they offer, of heaven as a waiting room or as a disembodied wind, are so bleak as to offer little or no real hope at all.

The third thing heaven is not is simply the reconstitution of our fleshly bodies. This is less of a mistake than the first two, and it may sound obvious in an age where cremation of dead bodies is relatively commonplace, but it's still worth stating. The funeral sermon that says, "I'm sure Peggy's up there now watering and pruning her roses just as she did down here" seems to be assuming that heaven is basically a continuation of our present physical life in all its prosaic mundanity. To be sure, heaven is a physical existence, but the bodies of the saints are not simply embalmed versions of the ones we have here. The idea of the Rapture is one that likewise overstresses the physical continuity of heaven. It's said in some circles that the Rapture is a good thing because it would whisk away all the fundamentalists and leave everyone else to get on with things, but that still distracts from the fact that the Rapture offers an impoverished picture of heaven.

So these are three things heaven is not. What's wrong with them is that they make no reference to the scriptural notion of heaven, have no place for God, and specifically have no relationship to anything brought about by Jesus. I wish I could say they were harmless, but I can't because, in fact, they detract attention away from the Bible, away from God, and specifically away from the God we meet in Jesus.

The Bible doesn't speak much about heaven as the eternal dwelling place of Christians. Instead it speaks of heaven as the place where God dwells, and this points to the crucial difference between a Christian notion of life after death and the ones I've been describing. For Christians, there is only one thing greater than the overwhelming horror of death, and that's the overwhelming glory of God. The popular verses I've quoted lose their credibility when they deny the overwhelming horror of death, and they lose any sense of wonder when they ignore the overwhelming glory of God. The Christian hope is that after death we come face-to-face with the wondrous power and love and passion of God, an experience we could liken to a tidal wave or a raging fire or a dazzling light, and yet, because of Jesus, that overwhelming glory doesn't destroy us, sinners that we are, but transforms us into the creatures God always destined us to be. After death, we face neither the oblivion of physical disintegration nor the obliteration of spiritual destruction but rather the transformation of glorious resurrection.

As we turn now to the three things heaven is, we realize that we find those things not by massaging our own bodies or souls for continuity but by looking to what we are shown of the character of God and by discovering that God's purpose is to model our transformed character on God's own character.

146

So the first thing heaven is about is worship. It's no coincidence that one scriptural picture of heaven is of a choir because a choir is a wonderful picture of what it means to have a body of your own but to find your true voice in a much greater body, a body where your voice sings most truly in harmony with the voices of others, where you find your voice most fully in words of praise and thanksgiving, where you are lost in concentration and where every detail matters, where you rejoice at the gifts of others that only enhance the gifts that are your own, where fundamentally you are all turned to face the source of your gifts and the focus of your praise. The reason we put so much care and attention into the way we worship at Duke Chapel is because we believe the way we worship is the most significant way we depict and anticipate the life of heaven. Every Sunday, Christians gather together and depict and anticipate the life of heaven. That's why worship matters so much: in eternity, that's all there'll be. Worship isn't just some abstract ideal. Everything depends on whom we worship. The book of Revelation makes it absolutely clear whom we worship—we worship the Lamb who was slain, the Lamb on the throne, Jesus, the one who gave his life because God loved us too much to leave us to oblivion and obliteration, the one whose resurrection gave us the life of heaven for which we long and on which our hope depends. What we strive for in worship is that every ounce of our energy and concentration is focused on the God we find in Jesus Christ so that we are truly lost in wonder, love, and praise because that's what heaven is like.

Here's the second thing heaven is about. Heaven is about friendship. Jesus said at the Last Supper, "I do not call you servants any longer. . . . I have called you friends" (John 15:15). The heart of God is three persons in perfect communion, and yet at the table there is a fourth place, a place left for us to join the communion of Father, Son, and Holy Spirit. This is heaven: the experience of being invited to the table of friendship to join the Father, Son, and Holy Spirit. At last we discover not just what God can do when left to do it on his own but what is possible when, in perfect communion, humanity and all creation join the everlasting dance of the Trinity.

If friendship is what heaven is about, that means not just friendship between God and us but friendship between us and one another. This is what the book of Revelation points us to when it talks at the very end of the coming of a new heaven and a new earth. At the very end of the Bible, we have this picture of Jerusalem the new city, coming down from heaven. In other words, cities are not essentially transitory, dirty, soiled things that are transcended by the coming of heaven. There will always be a city. Learning to live together as friends is at the heart of preparing for heaven, just as worship is. The reason we at Duke Chapel are working as hard at our relationship with our university and our city as we are at our worship is because we believe that making friendships across social barriers is what we shall spend eternity doing and that what we are called to do now is to anticipate heaven.

The third and final thing heaven is about is eating together. This is maybe the most common picture of all in the New Testament—heaven as a great feast, a banquet celebrating the marriage of heaven and earth, the perfect union or communion of God and all God's children. Just imagine a fabulous meal where there are no allergies, no eating disorders, no inequalities in world trade, no fatty foods, no gluttony, and no price tag. The reason the Eucharist is at the center of the life of Duke Chapel is because the Eucharist is where food, friendship, and worship all come together. We are made friends with God and one another when we eat together in worship. In eating together, we recall the transforming meals Christ shared before, during, and after his passion, and we anticipate the great banquet we shall share with him. The Eucharist depicts what creation was for and what it cost. When we gather together as two or three or twenty or two thousand and make new friends by eating together, we are celebrating a little Eucharist, a little icon of the Trinity at table together, a little glimpse of heaven.

This is what heaven is: worship, friendship, and eating together. Don't settle for anything less. Don't pass into the next room or become a thousand winds that blow. Don't leave the central claims and shape of the Christian hope behind you in the face of death just when it really matters. Enter the life that God has prepared for you, the life that Jesus laid down his own life to open up for you. Remember that Advent is about anticipating heaven, and spend your Advent getting your worship right, your friendship right, and your eating right.

There are things I haven't talked about. I haven't talked about whether heaven comes to us on the day we die or whether we await our resurrection on the last day. I haven't talked about near-death experiences and whether they tell us anything about life after death. I haven't talked about how we preserve our individual identity and personality when we've been so thoroughly transformed. I haven't talked about whether the end of the world is coming soon or is millions of years away. I haven't talked about them because I don't think, finally, they matter all that much. Like the popular verses, they're all about us; whereas what we'll discover is that heaven is all about God. There's a great sense of mystery about heaven, but I think the Scriptures tell us all we really need to know. They tell us what matters. What matters is being overwhelmed by the power and love and glory of God, now and forever. Heaven isn't a halfhearted reward for those who have lived a life of grudging misery, and it isn't an automatic entry into a revolving door of thudding dullness. Heaven is being overwhelmed by the horror of death and then finding not oblivion or obliteration but a further overwhelming. This second overwhelming is an overwhelming by the glory of God. It's a transformation into the life that the Father gave us, Jesus lived, and the Spirit infuses in wondrous worship, loving friendship, and a feast of praise. That's what matters. In the end, that's all that matters.

Hell

I have never heard a sermon on hell. The subject seems to sit grumpily and impolitely in the corner of the room, like a drunken uncle at a family Christmas dinner. This is an example of what I earlier called my "this looks like a tricky issue but let's bring the full theological resources of the tradition to bear on it" type of sermon. The message lies partly in the conclusion but just as much in the confidence it offers that no subject is too prickly or too dangerous to address in theological terms. Here I quickly establish the ground rules: God is good; God is almighty; the Scripture gives us some striking imagery; Jesus has changed everything. It is thus an attempt to train the congregation to think theologically. I find people respond extraordinarily positively to theological sermons like this. Many are used to bland commentary on life's transitions, detailed explorations of scriptural passages that still seem far away, or outspoken opinion on matters of topical interest, but a genuinely theological sermon, bringing resources the news media seldom employ about existential issues beyond the daily scope, seems to be exactly what many laypeople are looking for in a sermon, if they are looking for anything at all. As a preacher, one really has to search one's own heart and mind to address this kind of question, but the discipline is well worth it.

If there's one thing we believe in in America, it's choice. Last week I preached about heaven, and I sensed a consensus around the Chapel that heaven was rather a good thing. But as the days of the week go by, one's bound to think, surely there must be an alternative? Surely heaven can't have a monopoly? So this week I thought we'd have a look at that alternative. It's called hell.

There are good reasons for believing there's such a place or experience as hell. Most obviously, Jesus seems to refer to it a number of times, in the language of gnashing teeth, weeping, and the fiery furnace. Of course, the book of Revelation is particularly vivid in its portrayal of the lake of fire and its contents of burning sulfur. The existence of hell underwrites a whole moral universe, in which those who have shunned the light and truth of Christ and the gospel and particularly those who have made life a living hell for others on earth reap the rewards of their evil deeds. Those who turn to God in anger and dismay when cruelty and malice seem to prevail can find a certain comfort that not only are the good vindicated on the last day but the evil are soundly punished.

There are broadly three ways of conceiving of hell. The first is the endless, bloodthirsty torment of body, mind, and spirit that has captured the religious imagination over so many centuries and is the stuff of nightmares, graveyard humor, and revivalist preaching. This version sometimes appears with significant exceptions; for example, it's relatively common among advocates of eternal damnation to have get-out clauses for infants, for those who have never had a chance to hear the gospel, or even for those who have been faithful adherents of other faiths.

The second kind of hell is a modified version of the first. It makes a distinction between the references the New Testament makes to hell as a time or place of agony and remorse, and the somewhat fewer references in which that time or place of agony and remorse is described as permanent. The modified notion of hell sees it as a finite time of punishment or preparation, sometimes known as purgatory.

The third kind of hell recoils from the traditional emphasis on physical torment and sees punishment as simply annihilation. After death, those who are written in the book of life go to eternal blessedness while those whose names are not to be found in glory simply drop out of existence. They don't rot or scream or curse; they just cease to be. A modified form of this annihilation proposal is that hell is the experience of the absence of God. This is a mixture of the first kind, the agony and remorse, with the third kind, the oblivion and obliteration. The absence of God is truly eternal hell, but it seems to spare those with refined tastes of the grisliness of howling screams and boiling oil.

There are two main reasons why hell is a theological and philosophical problem. The first we could call the moral objection. What kind of a god takes delight in consigning people to eternal damnation? Is it possible to imagine the God who formed us and called us and came among us and transformed us turning around and consigning us to perpetual horror? At the very least, there seems to be a problem of proportionate response here. However ghastly the crime (and the twentieth century saw a good number of atrocities), surely it could be paid off after the first fifty million years in hell? Isn't eternal punishment a little excessive? It's hard to see how anyone could be happy in heaven forever knowing that eternal damnation was still going on downstairs.

The second objection to hell is what we could call the sovereignty problem. If God is all-powerful, how is it possible that things ultimately turn out differently from the way he wants them to go? Once we have ruled out the vindictive, merciless picture of God and thus assumed God wants all people to go to heaven, the suggestion that some never make it presents a major theological problem. How could God allow some aspect of his creation somehow to be lost forever? It's no use saying this is about free will because it's simply not possible to imagine anyone choosing eternal damnation, however limited the rest of the menu and however unstable or antagonized he or she was at the point of choosing.

These two philosophical objections to hell are pretty over-whelming because they strike at the two most fundamental Christian assumptions about God—that God is all-loving and all-powerful. The existence of hell implies that God isn't all-loving (otherwise, he couldn't consign parts of his creation to eternal damnation) and that God isn't all-powerful (otherwise he'd be able to bring their torment to an end whenever he saw fit). The notion of eternal hell implies not just that there comes a point where we can't change our mind but that God is as constrained as we are.

I think we should be wary of the first objection. There's always a danger of reducing God to our own size. It's obviously a mistake to project onto God all our anger and frustration and assume God gives the people we don't like a really hard time forever. It's also dangerous to concoct a list of polite and genteel and fashionable virtues and say God is just a big version of that list. God is our definition of good. If there is a hell, we have to believe that's all part of God's loving economy, whether we understand it or not.

The logic of the second objection is a whole lot more convincing. The major flaw in arguments for hell is that they take evil so seriously that they make it more significant than good. The reason I don't talk more about the devil is because the devil always ends up sounding more interesting than God. And I want to talk about God. At the heart of God is Jesus. And Christians believe that in Jesus, particularly in his death and resurrection, God defeated sin, death, and the devil. The existence of an everlasting hell suggests, however, that there is something God didn't defeat in Jesus—some part of eternal existence that continues to hold out against God, a part of God's economy that refuses to abide by God's grace. Again, it's no use saying this is a matter of free will, that if people weigh the pros and cons and opt for eternal damnation then God loves them enough to let them go. That would be putting human choice at the center of the universe, instead of God's grace. Surely the character of God's grace, the wonder of God's grace, is that God finds a way to draw back into his glory even those who are dead set against his kingdom and his love. The heart of the problem of hell is that it suggests God didn't achieve everything in Jesus, that the gift of Jesus didn't somehow give us everything we need, that there's still somewhere a fundamental, eternal estrangement from God.

So how do we listen obediently to the words of Scripture that speak of fire and torment and gnashing of teeth and, on the other hand, believe not just that Jesus shows us the character of God but that God achieved everything in Jesus? I suggest the key lies in today's words from the prophet Malachi: "But who can endure the day of his coming, and who can stand when he appears? For he is like a refiner's fire and like fullers' soap; he will sit as a refiner and purifier of silver, and he will purify the descendants of Levi and refine them like gold and silver, until they present offerings to the LORD in righteousness" (Malachi 3:2-3). I want you to think about this picture of a refiner's fire.

I want you to consider that the line between good and evil lies not like a thread through society, between good and evil persons, those destined for heaven and those destined for hell. I'd like you to suppose instead that it goes through every single human being, and I'd like you to imagine that there is indeed a fire that burns, not eternally, but until the last day and that after we die every little piece of us that has not turned to the glory of God, every tiny part of our history or character, every word or thought or deed that shrinks from God's grace is burned off by the refiner's fire. This means that when that process is finished, not all of our earthly self gets to heaven, but not none of it, either, even among the worst that humanity has produced. Out of such as remains from the refiner's fire, God remakes a heavenly body fit for worship, friendship, and eating with him forever.

For the Mother Teresa and the Francis of Assisi, we can imagine that there's very little burnt off and the refiner's fire is pretty much a painless process. They have accepted the forgiveness of God and been transformed by the sanctification of the Holy Spirit. They're pretty much in the clear, and in heaven they'll be instantly recognizable. But the Adolf Hitler and the Joseph Stalin are another matter. Almost everything in them, so we imagine, turned away from the grace and transforming love of God in Christ, and forgiveness was something they never sought. But here's the twist. Because God created them, because they emerged from God's creative purpose, we cannot simply say they are evil without giving up on the all-pervasive grace of God. So what we say is that for people like them the refiner's fire is an agonizing and almost total experience and that what's left is pretty much unrecognizable. It takes God to the very limits of his grace to make something beautiful and heavenly out of the scant and desolate remains that emerge from the refiner's fire. What does appear in heaven after God's astonishing work is almost unrecognizable from the earthly person who perpetrated so much that desecrated the name of God.

So that's what hell is. Hell is not an eternal horror that abides forever as a scar on the face of God's glory. Hell is a refiner's fire from which everything in us that has been soaked in God's forgiveness and transforming sanctification moves on quite rapidly, but it is a refiner's fire in which everything in us that has turned away from the glory of God remains, being prepared to meet God for as long as it takes until the job is done. The punishment—if that's the right word—for the Hitlers and the Stalins and indeed for everything in each of us that we call sin is that by the time it gets to heaven it's unrecognizable from its earthly self. And the less you allow yourself to be changed by the grace and transforming love of God in this life, the more agonizing and more radical the change will be when you leave this life.

Where is Jesus in this refining fire? The answer is that Jesus is at the heart of the refining fire. Can you imagine that the work of the refining fire is easy? Can you imagine what it costs God painstakingly to eradicate everything in us that turns from him and even more painstakingly to reconfigure a new person based on however little is left after the fire? This is to take on total alienation from God and try to transform even that alienation into something beautiful and glorious and truly heavenly. This is exactly what Jesus wanted to say no to as he knelt in Gethsemane. This is exactly what took Jesus to Calvary. This is exactly what was taking place on the cross. Jesus literally went through hell for us. Jesus on the cross was taking upon himself all in each one of us that turns away from the glory of God—all the sin of the world.

On the cross, Jesus was in the refiner's fire, burning with agony so that he could refashion each one of us for heaven. The astonishing thing is that in Jesus God doesn't just enter the fire and make something wonderful from our ordinary and limited humanity. God even makes something out of the ashes. Somehow, once the fire has done its work, God in Christ transforms even the lost. In the resurrection, we see in Jesus God's grace and commitment to give each one of us a restored and transformed identity once the refiner's fire has done its work. Even the risen Jesus wasn't identical to his precrucifixion self. How much different many of us may be. Because of Jesus, hell is not God's last word on sin, so the more we focus on the cross, the less we think about hell. Jesus really did change everything.

This is a picture of hell that stays true to the scriptural imagery, stays true to our faith in the self-giving and loving character of God, and stays true to our belief in the almightiness of God. Most important, it brings us closer to the wonder of what God gives us in Jesus Christ. This is a faith that leaves us not trembling in agonized fear or cozy in judgmental complacency, but lost in wonder, love, and praise. That's a big part of how we know it's true.

I want to do something I don't usually do, and finish with a prayer. It's a prayer that unites the theme of this week's sermon about hell and last week's sermon about heaven. It's a prayer that summarizes the intent of both sermons, which is to say that the way to think about heaven and hell is to focus on the God of Jesus Christ and not to settle for anything less. It's a prayer that I hope will become as precious to you as it is to me. So here goes: "Loving God, if I love thee for hope of heaven, then deny me heaven; if I love thee for fear of hell, then give me hell; but if I love thee for thyself alone, then give me thyself alone. Amen."

The Way There

Preaching on the atonement is often controversial. While the creeds of the early and undivided Church take no view on the matter, Protestantism has chosen to get extremely agitated about getting the answer right. I have always found Palm Sunday a challenging day to preach. There seem to be too many conflicting things going on, one of which is usually a busy service with a universal desire for a shorter sermon. The question at the heart of it seems to be, "How does Jesus save us?" This touches on what I regard as the two most fascinating questions in theology, namely, "If we had not sinned, would Jesus have come anyway?" and "If Jesus had not been betrayed and crucified, would God have saved us another way?" I want to offer the congregation the kind of wonder that such questions evoke. But there is a lot of material to cover, so again I give the congregation a simple structure to digest the conventional arguments in this area. I then go on to offer an approach owing a good deal to the work of N. T. Wright and his identification of Jesus as the one who brings Israel out of exile. Like the previous two sermons, the underlying purpose of the sermon is to strengthen the congregation's confidence that in Scripture, in tradition, and in shared discernment in the church, God has given us everything we need to investigate all the mysterious questions of salvation. My harshness toward the conventional atonement theories arises not because I think we do not need them—we do—but because they incline believers to seek salvation without Israel and without the church.

Palm Sunday is a day of paradoxes. Jesus is a king, but he rides not on a military horse but on an agricultural donkey. Jesus is the toast of the town, but five days later he is executed. He is the darling of the same people who will soon afterward call for his blood. Palm Sunday is the first of eight days that shook the world and shake it still.

The question I want to explore with you is at the heart of the significance of these eight days. How does Jesus save us? I want to set out five historic and widely held answers to that question and explore what our answer to the question might be today.

The first answer to the question focuses on Jesus' birth. The key date is Christmas Day. It says that Jesus saves us by reenacting or "recapitulating" every aspect of our human existence, setting right that which was out of joint. Adam disobeyed God by eating from the tree, whereas Christ obeyed God by dying on the tree. Christ sanctifies every dimension of human life. We are saved because in Christ the corruptible, finite quality of human nature is joined to the immortal, incorruptible character of God and thus transformed. The crucifixion and resurrection show that Christ also transforms death, but the real moment of salvation is the incarnation itself.

The second answer to the question focuses on Jesus' life. This is sometimes called the moral theory. It suggests that we human beings are the audience for Jesus' life. In his kindness and generosity, in his ministry to outcasts, sinners, and the sick, in his close relationship to the Father, in his prophetic confrontation with those who kept people under oppression, and most of all in his selfless and faithful journey to the cross, Jesus offers himself as the one who transforms our hearts to follow in his steps in the way of sacrificial love. Think of the words, "my richest gain I count but loss, / and pour contempt on all my pride."[2] This theory is sometimes described as subjective because Jesus doesn't seem objectively to change anything about fundamental reality. It is we who are changed. The danger can be that Jesus simply illustrates what we already knew by other methods than revelation.

The third answer to the question focuses on the suffering laid on Jesus as he went to and hung on the cross. Here the crucial moment is Good Friday. The theory is that humanity had accumulated an unpayable level of guilt before God. Humanity therefore deserved eternal punishment. Through a unique act of grace, however, God sent Jesus to face this punishment in our place. This is often called penal substitution. The words of Isaiah 53 are very significant and echo through Christian history:

> Surely he has borne our griefs
> and carried our sorrows.
> . . . .
> he was wounded for our transgressions,
> he was bruised for our iniquities.
> . . . .
> The LORD has laid on Him the iniquity of us all
> (Isaiah 53:4-6, NKJV™)

It's important to note here that what's most important is that Jesus suffered. While his death is significant and the resurrection is not ignored, the theory rests so much on the necessity of punishment that attention often focuses chiefly on the extent of Jesus' sufferings. Our imaginations focus on how much suffering it would take to substitute for the sins of the whole world. A characteristically Protestant version of this theory is that Jesus suffered not so much for humanity's sins in general but for each individual's sins in particular. Such an objective view of salvation leaves an open question about whether one is automatically saved whether one believes or not.

The fourth answer to the question also concentrates on Good Friday but this time focuses on Jesus' death itself. Jesus is a sacrifice that sets right our relationship with God. In this view, the problem is essentially one of debt. The most influential view says that the debt is to God's honor. The failure of humanity to do justice before God creates a terrible imbalance in the moral universe. Humanity *must* pay the debt, but only God *can* pay the debt. Hence the God-human, Jesus. When Jesus dies, he repays the debt of honor with interest, and it is this interest, known as merit, that humanity can access through the sacraments and thus find salvation. This is a characteristically Roman Catholic view. An older version of this theory also focuses on Jesus' actual death but sees the debt as owed not to God but to Satan. In this view, Adam and Eve had sold humanity to the devil; thus God needed to ransom humanity the way one would redeem a slave. Jesus' death, however, while succeeding as a ransom and buying us back, was in fact a trick because Jesus rose from death and escaped the devil's clutches. Whenever we use the word *redemption* we hint at this ransom theory, but the theory has in fact been out of fashion for a millennium or so.

The fifth answer to the question focuses on Jesus' resurrection. If substitution sees salvation as decided in a law court, then this fifth view sees it as a battle. Death cannot hold Jesus; he destroys death and opens out the prospect of eternal life by rising from the grave. The resurrection of Jesus brings about our resurrection by dismantling the hold of death not just once but for all time. Again there's a significant ambiguity here about whether this resurrection model logically means automatic salvation for all. Either way, the key word is victory. This is the characteristic Eastern Orthodox view. It has achieved a revival in the West particularly among those keen to stress how Jesus' resurrection doesn't just save the individual soul but transforms whole societies by dismantling all the social, economic, and cultural forces that oppress people.

Looking at the five theories, I'm sure that many people here will have been encouraged at some stage in their Christian life to regard only one of the theories as the whole story and to distrust or disapprove of the others. I imagine there would be a similar number who would like to take the best bits of all of them and simply say, "If there's salvation coming from Christ, bring it on; I'll have as much as is going, please." It's important to say that there are scriptural texts that lend support to all five views, so anyone who's in the habit of promoting suspicion around any of these views will have the relevant scriptural texts to deal with.

I want to suggest today that there's a real danger with all five theories, and that is that they're theories. That's to say, they are disembodied constructs that pay little or no attention to the context and contours of Jesus' life. The single word that epitomizes the context and contours of Jesus' life is this: Israel. Most of the theories of the way Jesus saves us exclude almost all the circumstantial detail that makes up the Gospels. There's a good reason for that: these theories are trying to set forth ways in which any individual anywhere can find salvation in Christ. But the trouble is, the circumstantial detail *is* the gospel.

Let me explain. When you hear all these theories together, you get this picture of this agitated God, worried about his honor or scratching around to find some booty to pay off Satan, subject to some eternal law court that says what he can and can't do, or fixing some kind of heavenly imbalance as if it were a leaky roof. You see a picture of the Holy Trinity as either subject to some eternal rule of engagement that's not of the Trinity's own making, or gathered together in the boardroom scratching their heads over Adam's fall as if it were a hole in the budget. What's this got to do with the Jesus of the Gospels? Almost nothing.

Instead, the Jesus of the Gospels reenacts the story of Israel, going down into Egypt with Joseph like Israel did, beginning at the Jordan like Israel did, facing forty days in the wilderness like Israel faced forty years, calling twelve disciples like Israel had twelve tribes, and most of all assembling around himself and transforming those facing internal exile in Israel—the leper, the prostitute, the tax collector, the social outcast—just as he came to transform the internal exile of Israel which found itself under Roman occupation. Five hundred years before Christ, Israel had returned from exile not knowing whether it had learned its lessons about sin, redemption, and the character of God from its time in Babylon or not. Finding itself in Jesus' time living under internal exile, it seemed not. Jesus emerged from Galilee with resonances of every major player in Israel's history. He was the second Adam; he was the one righteous man like Noah; he made a new people like Abraham; he was the new Israel like Jacob; he went down to despair and rose up to save his people like Joseph; he led his people to liberation like Moses; he was the ultimate king like David;

and he was a healer and troublemaker like Elijah. By facing the way of the cross, he took the story of Israel on himself and went into internal exile among his own people. *Exile* names the unique condition in which Israel discovered that God brings liberation through suffering and that God is made known through and to Gentiles as well as Jews. The cross is Jesus' going into internal exile to bring his people home and change the ending of Israel's story.

The cross was not, I believe, inevitable. That I regard as the special poignancy of Palm Sunday. It might not have been like this. The cross was always likely, even probable, because this is what happens when the utter goodness of God is utterly vulnerable in the presence of the shortsightedness and cruelty of human beings. That's why Jesus predicted it three times, but I don't believe the cross was inevitable. Israel could have said yes. I can imagine that, if Israel had rallied behind Jesus, the nation might have experienced much of what Jesus called the kingdom of God. What a threat to Rome that would have been, not a threat of arms but a threat of a changed society. Israel might then have been subject to a collective cross at the hands of the Romans as transforming as the cross of the individual man Christ. Isaiah 53, the story of the suffering servant, would have applied to the whole nation after all. But by telling us that Jesus died practically alone, the Gospels make clear that this was utter rejection, that God's people put God to the ultimate test. Most wonderful of all, God turned that rejection into the ultimate demonstration of grace, at Easter turning brutal death into breathtaking glory, and at Pentecost, in the birth of the church and in its being clothed in the Holy Spirit, making available to the whole world the homecoming brought about through Christ.

This is, I believe, how Jesus saves us. Not through a decontextualized theory that posits a faraway God doing curious deals in the light of arbitrary codes of debt, justice, or honor, but through the Jews, God's everlasting love for them, and his love through them for all the nations and the whole creation. The church is that body of people who declare they want to be in continuity with this story, who in baptism accept that this story is their story, who know themselves to be in exile from God and see Jesus as the one who went into exile for them and who finally brings them home. The church is not a collection of individuals who make their own private arrangements about which theory of salvation they fancy and who join up with a bunch of others who favor the same one. It is those people who believe they are called to be the context of Jesus' story.

The church is called to demonstrate that salvation in Christ isn't just a theory. If we start with one or more of the five theories of how Jesus saves us, we'll be casting around for a church that gets our favorite theory right, but it should be the other way round. We should seek to embody in our church life such hopefulness, such faithfulness, such patience, such endurance, such forgiveness, and such truthfulness that could only be possible if Jesus has saved us. We should be a context that demands an explanation, a living mystery that invites scrutiny. We should be a people coming out of the exile of sin, of oppression, of estrangement, of fear, of suffering, of death. We should be a people helping to bring others out of the exile of despair, of loneliness, of regret, of humiliation. We should be a people who speak of the God who made himself known to us in exile, the God who went into exile for us, and the God who brought us home. We should be a context that demands an explanation. The explanation is Jesus.

In the Gospels, the context of Jesus' story is the disciples, the poor, and the authorities, who together make up Israel. For much of the last two thousand years, Jesus' identity and story have been presented as if they needed no context, and thus the church has been invisible. Today, it is we who are called to be the context of Jesus' story. We are some kind of mixture of the disciples, the poor, and the authorities. We must ensure that salvation in Christ is never just a theory. It's a reality. It has to be seen in context, and it could just be that that context, at the moment, doesn't just mean the Jews. It means us.

Notes

1. The authorship of this poem is uncertain. See http://www.poetry library.org.uk/queries/faps/#5.

2. Isaac Watts, "When I Survey the Wondrous Cross," *United Methodist Hymnal* (Nashville: The United Methodist Publishing House, 1989), 299.

7

Speaking the Truth about Economics

The Command Economy

This sermon, on Exodus 20:1-17, the Ten Commandments, was originally entitled "One Is Plenty." It explores a regular theme of mine, that God has given us everything we need. This is the thesis I defend in my book *God's Companions*. Some of the paragraphs here revisit the arguments set out there. The challenge with the Ten Commandments is to resist extricating them from their context as the heart of God's relationship with Israel. Rather than begin with the historical setting, a familiar opening to sermons but one I tend to find rather tedious, I introduce the Old Testament context once the contemporary significance of the passage has been thoroughly argued. In this sermon, I am trying to bring together a tender pastoral awareness with a challenging social message and to build up to a conclusion in which the two are inseparable. The Commandments are familiar but here I am trying to locate them in the context of the whole Bible, of the whole of God's relationship with us, with the whole challenge of faith. I steer away from humor here: I tend to find that searching pastoral engagement and humor do not always mix.

Do you think you have enough? "Enough what?" you may say. Enough anything? Do you think you have enough money, for example? Or do you always look longingly through catalogues of expensive goods and always drive a hard bargain when the sales assistant suggests there may be a little flexibility? Do you think you have enough time, or do you complain that life's too short? Are you always attracted to goods that do things quicker, do you lose your temper at the stop sign when the car in front won't drive ahead when it's time and you can't move until it does? Do you think you get enough love, or do you look jealously at couples who seem wrapped up in each other, meticulously count your birthday cards and despair at how few there are, and wonder why small furry animals prefer sitting in other people's laps to purring in yours?

If there's one anxiety most people can share, it's an anxiety about not having enough. It's just as well because the economy depends on people thinking they need just a little bit more. If the secret got out that men could meet beautiful women without driving sleek new cars or that families could be civil to one another without a tasty new breakfast cereal or that it's possible to have sophisticated personal engagements without a highly sophisticated gadget on which to note one's personal engagements, then not only the advertising profession but half of the manufacturing industry would go under.

The Ten Commandments dismantle this nagging assumption that there is not enough. Look at the eighth commandment: you shall not steal. Think for a moment about the psychology of stealing. I'm not talking about the people running nursing homes in New Orleans who broke into supermarkets when they ran out of food for their ailing residents. I'm not talking about desperation. I'm talking about the state of mind that says it doesn't matter that I fiddle with my personal expenses because Duke's a big institution and it can bear it, and anyway it makes up a bit for what they don't pay me. The state of mind that says I have to publish that data, even though it's someone else's research not mine, because I need to get tenure. That's stealing. Stealing is saying there isn't enough in the world and if I'm going to have what I need then someone else is bound to suffer. But God said, "You shall not steal."

Look at the fourth commandment: remember the Sabbath day. Think about the psychology of working every day. It has to be done, only I can do it, everybody is depending on me, there's not enough time, it's a competitive world out there, if I don't get this contract someone else will, if I put a bit more time in this proposal it will be perfect, I'm not clever enough, I can only make up for it with hard work, my parents aren't paying for my education so I can sit around all weekend. Breaking the command to rest is saying there's only one savior in this universe and it's me. There isn't enough time, but I might just pull it off. I have to save my career, I have to save the world. I can't stop. But God said, "You shall rest."

Look at the seventh commandment: you shall not commit adultery. We all know that adultery is more often a symptom than a cause, but the mind-set of adultery is simply that one is not enough. By contrast, marriage is the great proclamation that one is plenty. All is focused on a single other—another mind, another imagination, another myriad of experiences and energies and enthusiasms and enjoyments. Could one ever exhaust that person? One other person is always more than enough when you believe that that person will listen to you until you run out of things to say, when you trust that that person will wait for as long as it takes for you to understand why you are the way you are, when you realize that that person will always impute the best of motives to your actions however clumsy you feel inside. You don't need to grab the biggest piece of cake anymore because you are one body, and your spouse's eating it is as good as your eating it. You don't have to have all the witty punch lines yourself anymore because it's not a competition for attention that only one of you can win. You shall not commit adultery. One person is enough.

Look at the third commandment: you shall not make wrong use of the name of God. Think about what is in our minds when we do so. It's when the language at our disposal doesn't seem to convey the strength or depth of feeling in our hearts. We hear a ripping sound when we put on a treasured item of clothing. Our favorite sports team is losing, and the weakest player on the team misses a golden opportunity. We hang on the telephone for twenty minutes, and a voice says, "We value you as a customer and will be with you shortly." Somehow language seems inadequate to express the depth of our distress on these occasions, so we invoke the name of God. We make the holy into the trivial and thus impoverish the language. Whenever we exaggerate, we do the same thing. We say the truth is somehow not enough. Don't invoke the name of God against call center operators, and don't invoke God's name to make your life sound that little bit more eventful and interesting. You shall not make wrong use of the name of God.

Then there's the second commandment: you shall not make for yourself an idol. Surely the psychology of this is that God is not enough—not big enough, or at least not near enough. So I shall make a god I can relate to, a god my size—a car perhaps, a career maybe, even the scales that tell me how much I weigh. Now we're getting nearer the heart of the problem. There's an abiding anxiety that we don't have enough—not enough property, not enough time, not enough love, not enough language. But the heart of the matter is that we feel we don't have enough God. For all our hymns and services and prayers and moments of truth, God is not enough.

That's why the moment in which God speaks these words is so significant. Israel has come out of Egypt but is already beginning to wonder if it wouldn't have been better off staying. This is the moment when God in essence says, *I am the Lord your God, who brought you out of the land of Egypt, out of the house of slavery. I have met your deepest yearning, and have exceeded it by giving you the promise of a land to settle in. I have been with you in the darkness, listened to you in your despair, led you out of death, dispersed your enemies, guided you by my own hand.* I have set you free. *I am the Lord your God. The problem is not that I am not enough for you—it is that I am* too much for you. *Your imaginations are simply too small to comprehend me. What you don't know is that this is just the beginning. I am the creator of heaven and earth. I have set you free, but I will also be faithful to you through unimaginable betrayal. I will come among you myself in the form of my only begotten son. I love every creature I have made, but I treasure each one of you as if you were the only one. I forgive you even when you have let me down seventy times seven times. Can you* imagine?

No, you can't, can you? I can see you can't. You still fall into thinking I'm not enough. You get anxious, and when you get anxious you start wanting more gods, more money, more things. I gave you manna in the desert, far more food than you needed. You still collected on the Sabbath because you feared there wouldn't be enough. I gave you water in the desert, but still your thoughts were straying back to Egypt. If only you could let your imaginations go and enter the land I am promising you, and let me set you free.

But in the meantime, here are some rules to remind you of what matters most, that I am more than enough, that my abundance is always greater than your scarcity. Have no other gods: more of them means less of me. Have no idols: they will never be remotely enough and will lead you to forget that I am plenty. Keep the Sabbath: I will give you all the time you need. Look after your aging parents and don't steal; I will give you everything you need. Don't kill people; they are part of the everything I am giving you. Don't misuse language; yes and no will be enough for you.

Really it comes down to the first commandment and the last. Here are you, anxious, covetous, looking at all the fun they seem to have next door, the great parties, the great sex, the amazing children, the plentiful friends, the healthy bodies, the gorgeous golden retriever, and all the time feeling more and more impoverished, more and more deprived, more and more sorry for yourself, more and more trapped in your stunted imagination, more and more a slave. And here, says God, am I, meticulously creating you in all your intricacy and beauty, setting you free from the darkest of prisons, forgiving you time and again even when your greatest hatred is for yourself, and coming among you to be your companion in Jesus.

Just you, and just God. Face-to-face. That's the moment when God stretches out two hands and gives you the Ten Commandments, just like you were Moses. God says, *I have set you free. You may forget that. You may fall back into thinking or feeling that I am not enough. A lot of people do. So here are some gifts. They will help you remember your freedom. They will challenge your imagination to realize that I am a God of abundance, who gives you more than enough, far more than you could ever want or need, who created galaxies no one may ever see, who has depths of forgiveness no sinner may ever require, who gives you in Jesus more love than you could ever realize.*

And we take the gift from God's hands and we look into God's face and we say, "May these commandments be to me always a gift and never a burden. May they always remind me that you are the one true God who has set me free. Write these words on my heart so I never forget that you are always more than enough. For now I realize that, with you, one is plenty."

The Divine Economy

This sermon, on Luke 16:1-9, was preached at the Duke University Baccalaureate in 2006. The Baccalaureate is a fine occasion marking the passage of the graduating class. It is attended by five thousand people spread across three services and watched on a livelink by three thousand more. For this sermon, I am deeply indebted to Ched Myers and his work on Sabbath Economics—it is he who pointed out to me the distinction between the two economies (a phrase from Wendell Berry) and named them "mammon" and "manna."

Preaching on such an occasion requires an avoidance of christological themes since the mood of the service is broadly theistic, or what is sometimes termed "generic." The parables offer opportunities to reflect on the new world God makes possible, without in every case dwelling extensively on how that new world comes about. There is an almost obligatory basketball reference (to a last-second long-distance basket thrown by a Duke senior) and a good deal of fun to be had in acknowledging (in their presence) the financial contribution of the students' parents. Beneath the surface is the intense anxiety about the Lacrosse Case, which had surfaced six weeks earlier, and phrases such as "hiring an attorney" and "sacked on the basis of unsubstantiated allegations" alluded to this universally understood context without dwelling on it.

We've just listened together to a story, a story that's often called the parable of the shrewd manager. What I'd like to do with you today is to read that story three times—once as a story about a manager, a second time as a story about economics, and a third time as a story about you on your last day at Duke.

So let's begin with the simple story of the manager. It comes in four scenes. In scene one, we have a very wealthy man and a manager who is very wealthy too because he has the use of everything the rich man has. Quickly we move to scene two. In scene two, the rich man hears that the manager is squandering the property and straightaway fires him. We may be alarmed that this is a world in which the manager can simply be sacked on the basis of unsubstantiated allegations. But there is a moment of grace. Before he clears out his office, gets a sympathetic pat on the back from his staff, and takes home the family photos, the manager gets the chance to visit all the rich man's clients to settle up their accounts. And so to scene three, in which the manager has a bright idea. Rather than feeling sorry for himself or hiring an attorney, he sets about writing off the debts of the rich man's major creditors. It's too late to make money, but it's not too late to build social capital. He starts making friends, people who will be pleased to see him even when he's out of a job. In scene four, the rich man comes face-to-face with the manager, and the rich man says, "Good for you, you were in a mighty big hole, and you got out of it simply by being generous. You realized that generosity is the best investment. You're better at this than I am."

It's a simple story but a fascinating one. It's fascinating partly because it's a great escape story. We never tire of seeing whether Brer Rabbit or Huckleberry Finn or Indiana Jones can get out of a mighty big hole. We never tire of recalling what Duke's Sean Dockery pulled off in the last seconds against Virginia Tech. But it's fascinating also because it contains an electric shock at the end. What might it mean to live like that? What might it mean to hear a rich man say to you, "I can see you've discovered the secret of real wealth—generosity." Could it really be that generosity is the best investment? Has Wachovia heard about this? Has Alan Greenspan?

Let's read the story a second time, not so much as a simple story about a manager but with these larger questions in mind. Let's read it as a story about economics. So, in scene one, we have a stark picture of economic realities. One man has a huge amount of money. The story begins with him because he has all the power. Everyone else matters according to how they relate to him. He has a manager. In this kind of economy, you want to be a manager. You get to spend someone else's money as if it were your own, but scene two tells us all we need to know about the downside of this economy. It's dominated by sudden mood changes, by gossip and anxiety. The word goes round that the manager is doing a poor job, and snap, just like that, he's fired. There's no settlement package, no face-saving retirement party; he's on the street. There's no job security, no respect, no trust. Sure, there's a lot of money out there, but everyone is just a puppet on the rich man's string. Now, look what happens in scene three. The manager says to himself, "I wonder whether this is the only kind of economy going. I wonder whether in this desperate moment it might be time to try a novel approach."

What might this novel approach involve? Well let's start by looking at the root of the word *economics*. Economics is *oikonomia*—that's to say, it's Greek for "household management." *Economics* means putting your house in order, but what if you've lost your home, lost your job, lost your shirt in a cutthroat economy? Look closely at what the manager says to himself: "I have decided what to do so that, when I am dismissed as manager, people may *welcome me into their homes*" (Luke 16:4). Isn't that an interesting phrase? It's obviously important because it's repeated at the end of the story: *welcome me into their homes*. In other words, when my economics is up the creek, it may be time to invest in somebody else's. When my household is bankrupt, it may be time to think about other people's households. It's time to change economies.

The Jewish and Christian Scriptures have words to name the two economies portrayed in this story. The economy of the rich man is called mammon. It's fine as far as it goes, but the problem is that it doesn't go very far. It only includes certain people, only buys certain things, only lasts a limited length of time. Mammon is fundamentally the economy of scarcity. It is the world in which there is not enough to go round. Mammon means I must use all my energy making sure that of the limited amount of cake, at least I get enough on my plate. There's also a name for the other economy, the economy of the manager after he's been fired. The biblical word for that economy is manna. Manna is the food God gave to the Hebrews in the wilderness; it was always more than they needed. It only dried up when they tried to take two days' supply at once. Manna is for everybody, gives what money can't buy, and never expires. Manna is the economy of abundance. It is the currency of the kingdom of God. The secret of happiness is learning to love the things God gives us in plenty. The name for those things is Manna.

What happens in scene three of this story is that the manager gives up trying to squeeze people for a living and starts making friends instead. He realizes the friends are more important than the money or even the job. He moves from mammon to manna, from an economy of scarcity and perpetual anxiety to an economy of abundance and limitless grace.

And what happens in scene four? The rich man realizes that the manager's economy is bigger than his. The rich man, sharp as he is with the shekels, can spot a winning formula. He *doesn't* say, patronizingly, "You're a lousy manager, but at heart you're a decent guy." He *does* say, "I can see my economy is smaller than yours. You're the one who's living in the great economy. I need to learn from you."

Just take that in for a moment. This isn't a familiar bleeding-heart liberal versus hard-nosed conservative contest. This is two economies face-to-face. The manager's economy of friendship is just plain bigger than the rich man's economy of debt. The manager has left the rich man's economy, and the investments the manager has made have made him rich in a way the rich man can only begin to imagine.

And now to read the story a third time, as *your* story, your story on your last weekend at Duke before you leave to become shrewd managers. Let's go back to scene one. You are the manager. You have been living at Duke, like the manager, on other people's money—whether your parents' or financial aid or Wachovia bank. And here we are suddenly in scene two, on the day of reckoning. You're about to be cast out of this cozy world of ideas and study and sports and parties, out of the gothic wonderland, and you're about to face the cold, harsh reality of scene three. In scene three, you face a fundamental choice, a choice that is what this story is all about. And if you haven't quite grasped so far what it is, I'll put it quite simply: it's the economy, stupid. The choice is, which economy are you going to live in?

Are you going to live in the small economy, the economy that is fine as far as it goes but that turns out not to go very far, the economy that only includes certain people, only buys certain things, only lasts a limited length of time—the economy of anxiety and scarcity? Or are you going to live in the great economy, the economy where the only use of wealth is to make friends and set people free, the economy in which you are never homeless and you cannot be destitute because you have spent your time and money making friends who will always welcome you into their homes—the economy of abundance, where generosity is the best investment? Which is it to be? If you live in the small economy, you will spend your life fearing for your job, your livelihood, your reputation, your health, your family, your life itself. If you live in the great economy, you won't fear anything. You'll have the things that money can't buy, and you'll know the things that hardship and even death can't take away from you. You'll have learned to love the things God gives us in plenty. You'll be living truly abundant life.

And if you make that choice, then when it comes to scene four, everyone will want to know you, to learn from you, to imitate you. We could call scene four Judgment Day, but at Duke we have other names for it. We call it Alumni Weekend. We call it a bunch of friends meeting up for a drink in New York—or even a funeral. We call it slyly Googling the names of your old mates to see what comes up. One way or another, we see the people who were here at

Duke with us years before, and between the lines we discover which economy they've been living in all these years. When the word begins to get around that you've been living all this time in the great economy, there's a bit of a stir; and the undergraduates begin to hear about it, and even the faculty raise an eyebrow; and together they say, "We hear you've been living in a world where everything you had was turned into releasing people from debt, all your energies have gone to liberating people from disease, and all your passion has been spent on setting people free from despair. We can see you don't have much money, but you don't seem to need it because you're surrounded by friends. We'd like to be like you."

The Grace Economy

This sermon, on Revelation 1:6, was preached in the context of a service focusing on the university's and the chapel's engagement with neighborhoods and issues of social inequality. It is an unqualified attempt to offer a theological analysis of poverty. As with more pressing and topical questions such as Katrina and September 11, I see my role to be that of a theologian as well as a pastor and preacher. I want people to come to Duke Chapel expecting not just words of comfort or exhortations to action, but a confident and hopeful wrestling with the troubling and abiding issues that almost everyone ponders at some stage. If one can offer something conceptually simple but theologically sharp and suitably accessible, one is offering something that simply is not available elsewhere. I make a move in this sermon that is unusual for me, which is to offer a model (disease) that I acknowledge is unsatisfactory, but doing so enables me to critique other more familiar models with a certain humility, given the insoluble character of the issue. The occasion also marked reunion weekend, and rather than lean toward nostalgia, I chose to explore an issue that is as distressing today as it ever has been. As elsewhere, using a simple structure enables the sermon to run through some fairly detailed social analysis without losing the congregation. The original title was "The University, the Church, and the Poor."

Why are people poor? What can or should those who are not poor be doing about it? Those are the two questions I want to address this morning.

There are several reasons we might want to avoid talking about poverty. One is that talking about "the poor" means giving people a label, and that's almost always a mistake because it leads to treating people as objects, making their humanity invisible and thus increasing their poverty. Another is that there are so many party political flags in the ground that it's quite a challenge to slalom through them to a genuinely theological understanding. Another is that poverty seems such an abiding aspect of human society that engaging it feels depressing, guilt-inducing, and disempowering.

Despite these good reasons, people in churches and universities talk about poverty all the time. It's taken for granted that major programming will have a dimension that addresses poverty, and the Duke-Durham Neighborhood Partnership, PathWays at Duke, DukeEngage, and a host of campus ministry and Congregation at Duke Chapel initiatives express this assumption. While most modern universities are ambivalent about religion in general and a little bewildered by Christianity in particular, the social outreach part of religion is something most higher education institutions can digest fairly easily. We could call it the acceptable secular face of God. But what *is* poverty? Why do people become and stay poor? What can be done about it? These are questions we don't so often ask.

Let's start with the question, "What is poverty?" I'll introduce you to a woman from the two-thirds world called Maria. Why start with a woman? Well, women perform two-thirds of the world's work, earn one-tenth of the world's income, are two-thirds of the world's illiterate, and own less than one-hundredth of the world's property. Maria lives in substandard housing with inadequate sanitation. With little or no land, livestock, or spare cash, she doesn't have the means to feed herself regularly. She doesn't get enough nutritious food to give her a lot of energy and help her fight off infections. She doesn't live near places where goods are bought and sold or places where capital or credit is available. What money she is able to save is likely to be consumed by obligatory cultural rites of passage.

She lives in fear because she's so close to the edge that a natural disaster could force her to sell what few assets she has simply to secure short-term survival. She's easy prey for the forces of exploitation, the moneylender, the protection racketeer, the merciless landlord, the bogus holy man, the drug dealer. Under pressure on all sides, her key domestic, extended family and community relationships become fragile, and she is isolated from trustworthy people on whom she can rely. Deprived of the trust that is at the heart of faith, it's hard for her to hear or believe in the utter and endless love God has for her. This accumulation of circumstances leaves her powerless. It's hard for her or anyone meeting her to identify what she's done wrong, and it's hard for her or anyone meeting her to identify exactly what a willing person could do to help. This is poverty.

Such a description of poverty shows how many of the issues cross over from the two-thirds world to the developed world. A person in Durham can share most of these experiences with Maria. While universal education is a massive opportunity, in many cases the other pressures of life that I've just been illustrating make it hard for a child in poverty to take advantage of that opportunity. It's worth noting that many of the characteristics of social isolation I've listed can confront those *with* money too. If your network of relationships becomes so fragile that you live in fear and can't trust any of the key people in your life, your bank manager may still say you're rich, but your experience may be so damaged that poverty might seem a good word to describe it. In that sense, poverty really can come upon anybody.

The question of why people become and stay poor is a controversial one, to say the least. It's a huge subject, but I'm going to suggest that there are three key metaphors that dominate a lot of thinking about it.

The first is the metaphor of the desert. People are poor because they don't have enough. They don't have enough money, food, good relationships, skills, education. This isn't really anyone's fault. It's more about a problem of scarcity of resources or poor distribution. The solution is to give people more—in the short term, more nutritious food and clean water; in the long term, more education, more training in sustainable agriculture and healthy work and family patterns, more stable institutions, more access to credit, and more outlets for their skills. The desert metaphor motivates many nonpoor to active involvement in relief and development, but it can lead to a quasi-colonial attitude that misses people's humanity. It can assume an us-and-them where "we" are defined by what we have and "they" are defined by what they lack.

The second metaphor is favored by those who are disillusioned or angry about the naiveté of the desert metaphor. They see the problem as not about scarcity but about sin. This second metaphor is that of the prison. Poverty is a kind of incarceration. Many see poverty as a prison into which people are put by others. They see the poor as kept in poverty by a widening circle of exploiters: by the local nonpoor who siphon off resources and benefits that were intended for the poor, by local authorities who use blackmail and violence to rob the poor, and by local employers and traders who use their strong bargaining position to force the poor to sell their goods and labor for far below market value. Others see poverty as a prison in which people put themselves, either by passive characteristics such as laziness or lack of ambition or by more active destructive tendencies such as reckless behavior or substance addiction. The prison metaphor motivates many social justice and evangelistic responses, but it can get so caught up in social theory or theological paternalism that it can, like the desert metaphor, miss people's specific humanity. It can overlook the extraordinary ingenuity required to live in poverty and demonstrated by those poor people who survive.

The third metaphor sees poverty as disease, as a kind of sickness. Disease is usually not something you're born with but is something you can quickly pick up from those around you. Disease is a kind of compromise between the metaphors of desert and prison. To use this metaphor, one must always remember that the sickness lies fundamentally in relationships, communities, and societies rather than in individuals. I think, despite the stigma of the word *disease*, it's still potentially the most helpful metaphor of the three. Unlike the prison metaphor, the language of disease isn't about blame, but unlike the desert language, it takes the complexity of poverty seriously. Disease language helps us recall that poverty, in some of its dimensions, can afflict even the circumstantially rich. A disease is a condition with a nonhuman root cause and physical, mental, social, and spiritual symptoms, which nonetheless require a very human response in every dimension. Like the reaction to any other disease, that response is sometimes aimed at identifying and facilitating a cure and sometimes focused on continuing to care when a cure is not perceivable. Either way, it's about balancing the general characteristics of the disease with its particular manifestation in each person and community and realizing that physical change is only part of an ecology of relational, spiritual, and communal dimensions of healing.

What does it mean for a university to address poverty? This is a pressing issue for many people in a place like Duke. It's a question for the Duke-Durham Neighborhood Partnership and for many of Duke's departments, institutes, and schools, such as Public Policy, Political Science, Divinity, the Community Service Center, and the Council for Civic Engagement. If one takes the first metaphor and sees poverty as desert, the tendency is to see Duke as a place with lots of resources and to assume that addressing poverty means simply transferring resources from one location to another. If and when poverty continues to exist, the logical explanation is that not enough resources have been transferred. This shows the inadequacy of the desert metaphor and the kind of thinking it leads to. Poverty is much more complex than simply one set of people having fewer resources than another. If one takes the second approach and sees poverty as a prison in which the poor are put by the machinations of the nonpoor, conscientious efforts to address poverty on the part of the nonpoor will seem to be no more than sinister public relations exercises, claiming goodwill when all the while underwriting oppression. While such analysis may sometimes be healthy correction from a critical friend, it seems to me more often to perpetuate a self-fulfilling cynicism. One may take the third approach, however, and see poverty as a disease by which *some* are afflicted but by which *all* are diminished. From the perspective of affliction, initiatives such as neighborhood partnerships are ways of getting all the stakeholders round the table to evaluate local wisdom, pressing problems, and wider resources, while affirming and empowering local leadership, individual initiative, and shared responsibility. In other words, exactly what's required.

It seems to me the best way for a university to address poverty is by being a university. That is, on the one hand, to be a greenhouse of ideas and research into what works and what doesn't, what causes and what cures, what curses and what heals; and, on the other hand, to model what a genuinely healthy community might look like and what there is to live for once one has emerged from or been helped out of poverty. Being a good neighbor is important, and it's always worth underlining that there's no story of Durham that's not about Duke and no story of Duke that's not about Durham. The best thing Duke can do in relation to poverty locally and internationally is to investigate and codify global examples of transformation and healing and to model what it means to be a healthy community.

That brings us finally to the question of what it means for the church to address poverty. "The glory of God is a human being fully alive," said one of the early theologians of the church. The church is in the business of glorifying God by watching, accompanying, celebrating, and participating in the way God brings people to become fully alive. That means people using their full capacities, it means people living in healthy relationships, it means people rejoicing in faith in God, and all of these things through good times and bad. Anything less is a kind of poverty, and it's a poverty that can apply to anybody.

The church is called to be in such a relationship to the poor that the poor are no longer "other" and poverty is no longer an abstract noun. Many of the poor are part of the church, and all of the poor are close to God's heart. Being a Christian means restoring friendship with God, with one another, and with God's creation, and that has to include restoring friendship between the nonpoor and those who are poor, or in some cases making overtures and adventures in friendship where no friendship has gone before. If we think of poverty as a kind of affliction, then the church's efforts should be divided between helping the afflicted find healing and walking alongside them whether they find healing or not. The testimony of the saints is that this is precisely where riches are to be found. Riches are to be found in walking with the poor, in sharing the joy of coming out of poverty, and in making the discoveries and the friendships that bring surprises even amidst poverty. As the Chapel and Congregation have been discovering in the new friendships we have been making in Durham's West End and elsewhere, riches are not to be found in sealing oneself off from relationships that will demand, challenge, or threaten one's affluence. That is simply to impose on oneself a different kind of poverty.

Riches are to be found in discovering our role as priests. We read in Exodus that God called Israel to be a priestly kingdom. In

Revelation, we read that Jesus "loves us and freed us from our sins by his blood and made us to be a kingdom, priests serving his God and Father" (1:5-6). A priest is one who takes the gifts of the people and celebrates as God transforms the gifts of some into his blessings for all. A priest is one who takes the sins of the people and rejoices as God transforms the poverty of our nature by the riches of his grace. This is what it means to be fully alive, and this is what it means to glorify God. Protestants can be a bit wary of the word *priest* because it sounds a bit Catholic and churchy. But those of you here today as alums, do you not look back on your life and say, "This is what I've been trying to do all along, to take the gifts I've been given and let God transform them into blessings for all, to take the problems I have found and ask God to turn them into his opportunities"? And don't you look back and see the glory of God? And those of you with your careers ahead of you, isn't this what you long for your life to be about? This is the way in which we are all priests, a priestly kingdom. And this is our prayer for the poor, that they may discover and we may discover from them how to be priests, to turn resources for one into blessings for all, to turn adversity into an occasion for intimacy with God, to turn even sin into a discovery of the transforming grace of God.

It's often recalled that Jesus said, "For you always have the poor with you" (Matthew 26:11). But it's often forgotten that when Jesus said those words, he was poor. What do those words then mean? I suggest they mean, "You will always be with the poor." For that is where true riches lie.

8

Speaking the Truth about Sex

Promiscuity

This was not a sermon but an address to an audience of Duke University alumni/ae on their reunion weekend. It is principally concerned with helping grandparents understand their grandchildren. The structure of the address imitates the three-chapter story outlined in the introduction to this book. One of the many challenges in talking about sex is to overcome the assumption that the preacher's first word is always to condemn. What I am seeking to do in this address is to portray three parallel worlds all existing on a college campus at the same time. I also seek to put the burden of responsibility on the listener, rather than allow anyone to develop a self-righteous attitude to a very complex subject.

They say politics, sex, and religion are best avoided at dinner parties, so I thought I'd talk about all three. I want to suggest that whatever has happened to people's expectations about sex in the last sixty years has more to do with politics than religion. Here's why.

For a large and influential minority of students today, sex is a sport. It largely happens late on Thursday, Friday, or Saturday night. It's mostly about casual one-night stands, preceded by heavy drinking and followed in the morning by—almost nothing. How has this culture come about? I suggest a story in three parts.

Let's start with what I'm going to call period one. Its definitive dates are 1929 and 1941. The first is the year of the Wall Street Crash. It symbolizes an era where economic well-being is always fragile. The only way out of poverty is hard work and a stable family life. Family is the only reliable insurance policy against the vagaries of health and old age. The year 1941 is the year of America's entry into World War II. This is an era of duty, where one's own needs and desires are secondary to a compelling greater national or moral cause. Think of the novel *Anne of Green Gables* or the movie *Brief Encounter*—women may study and spread their wings, but duty calls them back to the schoolroom and home, and passion is a fleeting fantasy suppressed by commitment to decency and order.

The year 1963 epitomizes the transition to period two. According to the poet Philip Larkin, sex began in 1963 between the Chatterley trial and the Beatles' first LP.[1] If *Lady Chatterley's Lover* taught the world anything, it was that sex was for women too. Put this together with the greater economic affluence of the 1960s, the widespread student revolt, and the civil rights movement, and we have many of the ingredients that led to romance taking over from economic security and duty as the primary matrix of sexual discourse. But the key development was of course the Pill. Add the year 1973 and the *Roe v. Wade* decision on abortion, and the revolution is complete: sex without guilt and sex without consequences become an intoxicating combination. Yet in the paradigmatic 1970 film *Love Story*, boy meets girl, they go to bed, they marry, she dies, he is devastated. This is still quite a conservative model. The economic and social revolution has taken place, but its logic hasn't fully worked its way through to the aspirations of the undergraduate. Sex may be easy, but a whole lot of people go away to college hoping to meet The One they will love and marry. A great many marry straight after college, and the economic demands of marriage and often family with relatively little income provide their own harsh economic logic.

The two dates that shape period three are 1983 and 2004. The former is the year AIDS became a household word; the latter marked the publication of Tom Wolfe's *I Am Charlotte Simmons*, a novel about so-called "Dupont" (with its imposing Gothic tower and top-ranked basketball program). Period three is a curious, and in some ways rather unattractive, combination of features of periods one and two. Needless to say, it shares period two's easy access to sexual congress, but romance and permanent relationships are no longer the aspiration. In Tom Wolfe's words, "At Dupont, nobody asked anybody out on a date unless they were already spending most nights in each other's beds, and even then the boy would word it along the lines of 'Whatcha doing tonight? Wanna chill?'"[2] One could say that in the seventies you went to parties to meet a partner, while today you don't settle on a regular partner because it would stop you going to parties.

Notice the subtle economic links between period three and period one. In period one, marriage and family stability were essential for economic security; today they are deeply problematic precisely because they jeopardize the individual's geographic and social mobility that is so essential for climbing the professional ladders that a college degree sets up. How can you stay together when his job takes him to Rome, yours to Tokyo? Marriage, or long-term partnership, becomes an issue much later when a career is established and the practicalities of home and children expose the loneliness of the isolated consumer lifestyle. Those who rushed into marriage in period two now find their children seem to spend their twenties still dependent on the parental home and bank balance for help during transitional moments of a life shorn of both duty and romance.

It's important to mention three things the pastor must always bear in mind in the contemporary sexual climate. The first is, never to suppose the current culture is without morality. It has its own very strict rules. For example, sleeping with someone from your own corridor or even hall of residence is widely frowned upon. Relationships where there is a significant power differential are also considered very dubious. Sexual violence is not publicly tolerated. The second pastoral guideline is, by no means is everyone living in period three. Always remember that the student body is made up of *people living in each of these periods*. (They always were; the novelist and philosopher Iris Murdoch, for example, was evidently living a period three lifestyle in the 1950s.) The first question to ask oneself if a young person wants to talk is, "Which period is this person living in? Are they dominated by duty and assuming virginity as a given (period one)? Are they longing to meet The One and open to letting their hormones do the talking if they sense they have done so (period two)? Or are they finding their way through the intricate social playground of period three?" The third guideline is, remember that behind each student is a parent—or two. Most Christian parents of my generation dream that their student offspring will inhabit period one, but parents are so overwhelmed by what they see as the nightmare of period three that they settle fairly happily if presented with period two.

Period three can't simply be dismissed as a den of iniquity or a cauldron of vice. It is the logical outworking of the political, economic, and social changes made forty years ago. Capitalism has made everything a commodity, including sexuality. In an intensely competitive marketplace, everything becomes a tool for social advantage, including sexual partners. Life at college is dominated by building a curriculum vitae, and the social scene is absorbed into the cultural pattern of acquisitive consumption. It is not just the partner who becomes a commodity: one is in the process of turning oneself into a consumer item, to be hired by an employer and sent around the world as the employer sees fit. Yet who knows how naive and virtuous period three may seem one day from the perspective of period four?

Christians may believe they have good news about the body, as a gift from God, destined for glorious resurrection and transformation, and a beautiful instrument for physically showing another person how deeply cherished he or she is by God. Christians may believe sexual expression belongs within a committed relationship defined as well by passion, permanent friendship, and hospitality to children, but Christians can no longer rely on social norms or economic necessities to shape sexual behavior for them. One can very easily fall into thinking that once there was a golden era when Christian assumptions about propriety were reflected in the general society's sexual habits. Whether or not this was ever so, it makes the mistake of thinking one can legislate or demand adherence to Christian patterns of life without communicating the convictions or practices that make those patterns meaningful.

Christians can no longer rely on economic hardship or a culture of guilt and shame to do the work of ensuring widespread adherence to their expectations about sex. They have to rely instead on their own witness and example. They have to live in marriages that inspire others, that survive and thrive through fondness, foolishness, and forgiveness, not through naiveté, self-righteousness, and prejudice. They have to offer models of a "good time" that go way beyond "getting wasted" and "getting laid." They have to portray a sense of corporate duty as compelling as that on offer in the fifties and a sense of passionate love as thrilling as that on offer in the seventies. Otherwise, no one is going to be much interested in what they have to say because what they have to say defies the economic, political, and social logic of the culture of which they are a part. And maybe that is no bad thing.

Adultery

This sermon was preached on the text 2 Samuel 11–12. I almost always follow the *Revised Common Lectionary*, so when it throws up a reading like this I feel bound to face the consequences. A sermon like this would be hard to preach if one knew three-quarters of the congregation well; it works much better when one knows about one-tenth of the congregation by name and perhaps another one-fifth by sight, as is the case on summer Sundays at Duke Chapel. The most uncomfortable line in this sermon is the one that includes the words "around half the people here today." People were lining up afterward to tell me that this was not their problem. I preach sermons like this on uncomfortable themes from time to time when the lectionary seems to insist on it; generally one morning early in the week I get a strong sense of God simply saying, "You have no choice this week; this is what you must do." By dividing the sermon between David and us, I not only get a chance to do some exegetical work on David, but I also get to say much harsher things about David than I do about the people in front of me. Having said so much so plainly, it felt right to change the status at the end and finish with words of pleading. The whole sermon rests on the assumption that the adulterer is not "other" to the people gathered that morning.

The story of David and Bathsheba comes at a key moment in the Old Testament. Up until this moment, one can read the Old Testament as a story of Israel's growing confidence and assurance of God's grace. Israel is given the law, by and large keeps it, and becomes a kingdom of great power and prosperity. This is the apex of the Old Testament, but after this moment, it all seems to go downhill. A fight over the succession leads to a split in the kingdom, and the two kingdoms in turn are invaded and humbled. Today's story is a kind of reprise of the Fall. David is like a rerun of Adam.

I'm going to read this story twice. The first time I'm going to talk about David; the second time I'm going to talk about you and me. This is one of the most uncomfortable stories in the Bible, so the next twenty minutes isn't going to be easy listening. Usually I judge whether you're engaging with what I'm saying by whether you're perfectly still; today I shall judge by whether you're shifting uneasily in your seats.

Let's start with David. The story has an opening scene that sets up a problem and then three scenes that seek to solve the problem. In the opening scene, David is at the height of his power, yet he is idle. This is the time of year when kings go out to battle, but David stays at home. His kingly office carries all the pressing affairs of state, but in mid-afternoon David is having a nap. With nothing much to occupy him, he wanders around looking for amusement or gratification. His gaze settles on a beautiful woman.

Idleness and power are a lethal combination. With nothing better to fill his time, David forgets what his power is for. His power is for keeping Israel faithful and keeping Israel secure, but he uses it for his own gratification. He ignores the fact that Bathsheba is still ritually unclean from her period. He ignores the fact that her husband, Uriah, is one of his best soldiers and, what's more, a sojourner in Israel who deserves special respect. David sets about possessing the woman, not forever but for now, not for sharing joy but for discharging lust, not to see her flourish but to hear her scream. Once used up, she's tossed back to her home. But there's one problem. She's pregnant.

David's first solution is to try to pass off the child as Uriah's. He brings Uriah home, gets him drunk, and tries to get him to sleep with his wife. You have to pick up the irony and the comedy in this scene. David is all-powerful, but try as he might, he can't persuade a manly soldier to go home and sleep with his stunningly beautiful wife. Uriah's priorities become simpler the drunker he gets; meanwhile, David's priorities become murkier however sober he remains. Look what happens to David. First he chats apparently normally to a man he has betrayed. Then he tries to persuade his faithful soldier to be less faithful and more selfish. Then he spends a whole evening trying to get his soldier drunk. David is getting more and more desperate, and more and more unscrupulous and more and more powerless. He is turning into a monster.

Having tried every subtle approach and failed, David resorts without hesitation to a ruthless and violent solution. He resolves to murder Uriah. Having forced Bathsheba to fulfill his desires, only for the situation to get out of control, he then finds Uriah can't be controlled and must be eliminated. Still eager to appear righteous, David gets his commander Joab to engineer Uriah's death in battle, but it turns out that quite a number of other soldiers get killed in order to make Uriah's death seem plausible. More and more people are becoming casualties of David's clumsy solutions. First a woman of the city becomes the tool of David's lust and idleness. Next David sets his kingly duties aside to work full time on engineering a cover-up. Then the whole strategy of the army is transformed into a system to dispose of a guileless husband. Idleness leads to lust, lust leads to deception, and deception leads to murder.

And so to a third solution. The prophet Nathan comes before David and tells him a story. A rich man had everything he could wish for, while a poor man had just one little ewe lamb, which he treated like his own child. When the rich man needed a lamb to feed a guest, rather than slay one of his own he took the poor man's precious ewe lamb. David is outraged. For the first time in the story he thinks of someone other than himself and considers a good that is more significant than satisfying his own desire and preserving his reputation. Compromised as his own situation may be, he sees this story as a straightforward matter of justice. Then Nathan says, "You are the man!" This story is your story. This situation is as straightforward as you could imagine. You are the man. David's secret is exposed. His outrage is turned on himself. He comes to his senses and says quite simply, "I have sinned against the Lord." At last, a true solution can begin.

That's the story of David. Now, how about the story of you and me? I'm aware of the limitations of drawing wisdom from an ancient monarch who already had several wives and a young wife of a soldier whose own wishes don't get a mention in this story. Nonetheless I'm going to draw five lessons from this story that may help us live more faithful lives. We're all sinners. Some of us commit adultery; many of us misuse power in other ways; all of us tie ourselves in knots of self-deception and draw others into our webs of deceit. What are we to do?

Let's start with David back home taking a nap in the afternoon rather than going out to battle like a proper king. He wants to go on being king, but he has stopped doing what kings do. He's heading for trouble. The best way to avoid sin is simply to have something more important to do. The time that faculty, careers staff, and campus ministers spend with students helping them plan their careers and discern their vocations is about helping them so fill their lives with worthwhile things that they won't have time to go astray. It's not about being busy for its own sake; it's about recognizing the massive need, overwhelming beauty, and remarkable goodness in the world and aligning one's own gifts and aspirations with those. There's more than a lifetime's occupation there for all of us. Perhaps the most straightforward reason for David not to take up with Bathsheba is that he didn't have time to.

That's not to say we don't need to develop self-control. David goes on the roof and spots a beautiful woman. There's nothing wrong in going up on the roof, but as soon as his desire starts to affect his judgment, he's heading downhill. What should he do? Quite simply, come down from the roof. And think twice about going up there again in the late afternoon. A woman once complained that it was so hard for her because a gorgeously attractive man got onto her train and sat there simply being irresistible. What could she do? A friend suggested simply, "Change trains." Change trains. Sometimes the simplest advice is the best. If you can't change trains, take a friend along with you. Recognize your limitations. Ask a friend for help if you're out of your depth. Don't put yourself in situations you can't resist. Don't go on the business trip with the gorgeous assistant. Don't go for the spontaneous drink after the late night meeting.

One of the things that restrains us from changing trains is self-pity. Most of us don't feel as powerful as David. For most of us, the temptation of adultery is not as much about the thrill of power as it is the illusion of powerlessness. We tell ourselves a story that we are not very attractive, not very interesting, and not very happy. We feel trapped and unappreciated. And then along comes this wonderful person who amazingly seems to regard us as beautiful, fascinating, and inspiring, so of course we sleep with this person. It's almost a way of saying thank you for appreciating me, but the real problem here is the false story we started off with. Most of us have far more power than we realize. Of course we listen if those close to us treat us with disdain and demean us. But the tragedy is if we only realize the power we have when we see the damage we can do.

The next thing David does is to assume sleeping with Bathsheba will be so fantastic that it's worth whatever it costs. One thing most of us never learn is that another person, fabulously beautiful or fun or interested in us as they may be, will never become that magical toy that fulfills all our desires. When we meet an attractive person, or spy him or her from a rooftop, that person becomes the vehicle onto which we project all our desires. To be cynical, one could say that most relationships last as long as each partner can keep up the appearance of carrying the other one's projections. This is expecting too much of another person, but it's also turning them into an instrument of our own fantasy. Before we are too quick to condemn David, we have to recognize that we each do this all the time. We are constantly disappointed when people fail to fulfill expectations they never invited us to place upon them. A real relationship is based on learning to love the real person once the fantasy has disintegrated, not just seeking a new fantasy. Pretty much everyone at some point in a marriage meets someone they would rather have married than the person they did marry. The only mistake is to think that's a big deal. David needs to grow up a bit.

The most positive thing for David would be to see this as an opportunity for reeducating his desire. There's nothing wrong in seeing a person, even a naked person, and saying to oneself, "I have just seen an incredibly beautiful person." The question is, what does one say and think next? Just imagine saying, "Seeing the beauty in this person makes me realize the beauty there is in every person, indeed in every created thing. This person is making me wake up to the wonder in the world. It is not that I admire him or her too much, but that I admire others too little. There are probably a thousand things in him or her that I should admire but haven't spotted yet. If I am drawn to him or her, I should become all the more aware of those astonishing things in each living creature, and even more sensitive to the glory of God's creation. If I really loved God with my imagination as well as my will, my interest in this person would be a very small part of my real desire. After all, desire is fundamentally a gift to lead us to God." David doesn't say any of this because he thinks everyone can become his tool. He turns every person into a toy and thus loses his wonder in God.

So here are some lessons we can learn in the face of disordered desire. Fill your life with such important things that there isn't time for distractions. If you're stuck on a train opposite a forbidden pleasure, consider changing trains. Don't tell yourself a false story that portrays you as the powerless one and forgets the damage you can do. Realize that every attractive person becomes a vehicle for your fantasies, and don't assume this new person is so special that you can suspend all logic. See this moment of temptation as an occasion to educate your desire, not to debase it.

So far, so good. But I'm not pretending these strategies always work, even with the wise, the farsighted, and the faithful. There's a lot of adultery around, and the statistics would suggest that about half the people here today know about it in their or their family's life all too well. Nobody can say this has got nothing to do with me. If you're a person who knows about adultery all too well, here are a few suggestions.

Number one, don't say it's the end of my marriage, my family, my world. Sometimes it does prove impossible to rebuild trust and hope and joy in a relationship, but it doesn't always turn out that way. Adultery is more often a symptom of trouble than a cause, and if both partners are committed to finding out together what the real cause is, it can become a new beginning. More than one person has said to me, "I can hardly believe I'm saying this, but I'm almost grateful for what she did because things are so much better now."

Number two, don't pretend this affair obliterates everything you previously knew about yourself, your partner, or the world. Adultery is fundamentally idolatry when you become so obsessed by another person you lose sight of all your other commitments. If you discover that your partner or you yourself have feet of clay, you haven't discovered the whole truth about the world, though it might feel like it at the time. What you've just discovered is that the gospel is more about repentance and renewal than it is about never getting it wrong and that we all desperately need God. Don't let it make you cynical. Don't let yourself be sentimental; you can't go through your whole life keeping everyone happy. Don't pretend you are powerless and there's nothing you can do to make things better. There always is.

And finally number three, don't think God cannot bring good even out of this. Don't flatter yourself that this is the greatest sin of all time. Don't pretend your sin is bigger than God's grace. If God brought good out of his son's crucifixion, he can bring something extraordinary out of your or your partner's foolishness and pride.

David got it badly wrong. He tried first of all to make it look as if nothing had happened. Then he tried to destroy anyone who stood to expose him. Finally he got down on his knees and said, "Sorry. I'm so, so sorry. I've been stupid, deceitful, selfish, and shortsighted. I can see that for a few moments of pleasure I've jeopardized everything else that I value. I want to begin the rest of my life from now. I want to learn how to love again, learn how to be faithful, learn how to let God speak through my weaknesses and shine through my brokenness. Please help me."

Homosexuality

This sermon was not, in fact, preached at Duke Chapel, but at St. Mark's, Newnham, Cambridge, UK, after the publication of the Windsor Report in October 2004. Because it was so widely circulated before and after I moved to Duke, I think of this sermon in the same category as my Duke Chapel sermons, and so it belongs in this chapter. On the Wednesday prior to preaching this sermon, I sent an e-mail message to a number of people in the congregation whom I felt had a particular interest in this issue or wisdom to bring to it. The e-mail simply said I was planning to address the question and I would welcome any suggestions or concerns. I tried to incorporate many of their reactions into the final version of the sermon.

The aim of the sermon is to encourage the loud proponents of various views on homosexuality in the church to see how much they need each other and to see the controversy as an opportunity for the renewal of the church rather than a cause of its division. The rhetorical technique involved is to allow the congregation to assume that, having set up four approaches, I am going to choose one of them; and then not to do so. The intention is that a sense of disappointment turns rapidly to relief and then quickly again to joy and hope. By carefully ensuring that the same amount of attention is given to scriptural warrants in each section and that each approach is given the same degree of affirmation and criticism, I am seeking to broaden the debate from its frequent polarized state. I am rejecting a split between the Bible on one hand and human experience on the other.

Of course this is by no means a comprehensive treatment. It would be interesting, for example, to add a consideration (prior to the "holiness" approach) of the understanding that there is no such thing as homosexuality as an identity and, likewise, to add a consideration (after the "liberation" approach) that there is no such thing as fixed sexual identity at all. While these might be more challenging to substantiate scripturally, they would transform the argument from one that presents four views in a spectrum to one that offers six views in a circle and thus shows that the logic of extreme "conservatives" and extreme "liberals" brings them curiously to much the same place. Leaving aside the limits of time, this would have taken me beyond a sermon into a lecture because it would have introduced playful and provocative elements that were outside my remit for that morning: to build up the faithful in appreciation of the gifts God had given them in one another.

I'd like to set before you four understandings of homosexuality. Each one is, I suspect, widely held in the church, and each one is represented in most congregations. I want to present each one in terms that its proponents would recognize. I will try to set out each argument at its best. For each of the four, I shall offer a summary sentence, a brief description, an account of its scriptural warrant, a comment on its strengths and weaknesses, a kind of nightmare vision if that argument were to go unopposed, a sense of what the argument might assume but not explicitly state, and one question I would like to put to those who hold that particular view. I am calling the four views, in order, holiness, kingdom, pastoral, and liberation.

The first approach says, "The Bible is clear." I'm calling this the holiness approach. This view rests on humility: Scripture offers us

God's pattern for human flourishing, and while certain things may appear to do no harm, one cannot seek a holy life while being unfaithful to the biblical text. The scriptural warrant comes from half a dozen texts. Leviticus is concerned with purity and the numerical growth of the population. It twice refers to lying "with a male as with a woman" as an abomination (Leviticus 18:22, 20:13). Meanwhile Romans is concerned with showing how not only Jews but also Gentiles have had the opportunity to follow God's ways, and it argues that men who were "consumed with passion for one another" and "committed shameless acts with men" are examples of departing from this natural law (Romans 1:18-32). In addition, 1 Corinthians 6:9-10 and 1 Timothy 1:8-11 include "sodomites" under a general list of lawlessness and profanity.

The strengths of this argument are its concern for holiness, its awareness of the need for discipline in the dynamic matter of sexual touch, and its respect for scriptural authority. It has several weaknesses. Its reliance on Levitical law leaves it having to explain why some laws in Leviticus are still considered valid while many are not. Even when the New Testament texts stand alone, it still has to explain why rules on homosexuality are inflexible while rules on divorce, usury, and the role of women seem to be able to change. It has to face up to an inconsistency in applying "single verse" injunctions. Why is the church not unambiguously pacifist? Why is it not committed to thoroughgoing simplicity of life? Why is it not committed to having goods in common? All these seem better grounded than an antipathy to homosexuality, but presumably they were found to be too inflexible if the church were to remain broad and socially sustainable. Meanwhile, some holiness advocates have an unfortunate inclination to using what I would regard as spurious "natural law" arguments that have little to do with Scripture—for example, that if we were all gay the species would die out, or that gay sex is unhealthy. There is also a tendency to use analogies that compare homosexuality to pedophilia. I regard all of these tendencies as weakening the holiness argument. However the most significant weakness is the very deep theological problem it raises. Many holiness proponents seem prepared to acknowledge that God makes some people homosexual, that homosexuality is a discovery not a preference, but this creates a troubling mystery of why God should do this. What kind of a God creates and bestows a gift then prohibits its flourishing? Thus the holiness approach seems simply to shift the problem from the Bible to God.

Underlying the holiness view is, I suspect, a sense that the world is getting out of control. It's sometimes said the church has lost the ability to speak about right and wrong: a stand has to be taken somewhere. That somewhere is often taken to be marriage. This is a view that carries widespread sympathy in the church. But I would point out again that it is not unambiguously derived from the New Testament, which seems more concerned with singleness and the body of Christ than with marriage. There is, meanwhile, a profound irony that many of those who want to protect marriage seem prepared to split the church. All the approaches have a nightmare vision. If the holiness approach were left to itself, the nightmare vision would be of a church self-righteous, legalistic, self-obsessed, constantly splitting, and dismissed by most progressive forces in society as hopelessly out of touch. The question I would want to ask the proponents of the holiness approach is, "Why has the issue of homosexuality become *the* issue?"

The second approach says, "Can we talk about something else?" I'm calling this the *kingdom* approach. This view draws attention to the main thrust of Jesus' life, preaching, work, and passion. He concentrated on bringing all kinds of people, especially outcasts, into his new kingdom. The kingdom approach maintains that homosexuality is a distraction from major issues like evangelism, war, abortion, poverty, money, and the environment. The scriptural warrant for this view rests on a simple word count. *Homosexuality* is not mentioned in the Gospels and has only a handful of references in the Bible as a whole; meanwhile, the issues the Gospels do talk about—use of wealth, loving God with all your heart, soul, mind and strength, and your neighbor as yourself, and simply following Jesus—are obscured by the focus on homosexuality. The radical Old Testament prophets simply ask that God's people "act justly, love mercy, and walk humbly" with God (Micah 6:8). This seems a lot more important than sexual orientation. Most gay Christians I know personally would be kingdom proponents, seeing their own sexual orientation as well down the list of the great issues facing the world.

The strength of the kingdom approach is its concern for the big picture and for the broad message of Scripture in the modern

world. Its weakness is that it has no positive argument on homosexuality. Not only is it eager to change the subject, it also makes
one feel one shouldn't be having the conversation. But bewilder-
ment is not an argument; impatience is seldom a good witness. If
the kingdom proponents have got nothing to say, they can't be surprised that the issues are being settled by others who have a lot to
say. A second weakness of the kingdom view is a tendency just to
ignore the parts of Scripture that don't fit its simple message. It
seems to struggle with the injunctions of Scripture that jolt the
assumptions of the twenty-first century. It forgets that discipleship
is about conforming one's world to Scripture, not conforming
Scripture to one's world.

Underlying the kingdom view is, I suspect, a desire for the simplicity of the direct response of the first disciples to Jesus and a
kind of resentment at anything that inhibits the straightforward
practice and sharing his good news. If the kingdom view were left
to itself, the nightmare vision would be of a church self-important,
impatient, depressed, and incapable of translating its noble ideals
into the day-to-day business of living and worshiping as a community. The question I would want to ask the kingdom proponents
is, "Might not what you see as a distraction in fact be inviting the
church to discover what it means to act justly, love mercy, and walk
humbly with God today?"

The third approach says, "Can't you see what the church is *doing*
to people?" I'm calling this the *pastoral* approach. The pastoral
approach seeks the virtue of honesty. It points out that there have
always been gay people in the church and in the priesthood, and it
maintains that it is high time to recognize the church as it really is.
It emphasizes concern for individuals. It is exasperated at the way
gay people are sometimes treated. It seeks that all people pursue
integrity, rather than what it tends to see as hypocrisy. The scriptural warrant is rooted in Paul's recognition that "all have sinned
and fall short of the glory of God" (Romans 3:23). This is in the
spirit of Jesus' words: "Do not judge, so that you may not be
judged" (Matthew 7:1). When Jesus was confronted with the
woman caught in adultery, he suggested, "Let anyone among you
who is without sin be the first to throw a stone at her" (John 8:7).
In the parable of the Pharisee and the tax collector, it is the one who
simply recognized himself as a sinner who went home justified,

rather than the one who was so keen to establish his righteousness (Luke 18:9-14). Jesus also said that what we do for the "least," we do for him (Matthew 25:40), and gay people have a claim to be regarded as the "least" in today's society.

The strengths of this argument are its emphasis on compassion, realism, and honesty. It reflects the widespread belief that if Christianity is about anything it is about love, and it asks whether there is really so much love in the world that the church can afford to stamp it down when it happens to appear. The weakness is its tendency to overidentify with individual concerns to the neglect of wider questions of church order and scriptural interpretation. The pastoral approach can be reluctant to articulate a corporate gospel distinguishable from tolerance and a respect for privacy.

Underlying the pastoral view is, I suspect, a sense shared by many in contemporary society, particularly of the younger generation, that large institutions are invariably oppressive and inhuman and that real value is largely or entirely to be found on a personal level, in the intimacy and trust of relationships and friendships. There is a tendency to seek in the church a haven from the hurly-burly of the aggressive, intrusive world. "Just live and let live" is the motto. Many of those who take the pastoral view might feel that even to preach a sermon on this subject is inappropriate. If the pastoral view were left to itself, the nightmare vision would be of a church that had given up on structures, had no overall vision, was entirely devolved, was concerned only to pick up the pieces, and had no mainstream agenda. The question I would want to ask the pastoral proponents is, "What genuinely constitutes a holy life for a gay person? Are privacy and tolerance really enough, or is it time to articulate a more constructive view, and does that mean celibacy, gay marriage, or some redefinition of sacred friendship?"

The fourth approach says, "This is a straightforward issue of discrimination." I'm calling this the *liberation* approach. The liberation view sees the question in terms of rights and justice. It sees discrimination against gay people as rooted in ignorance, prejudice, and the misuse of power. It believes the church should regard secular aspirations on rights issues as its own minimum standard. It finds the church embarrassing and way behind the times. It approaches Scripture in two ways. On the one hand, it insists that what Paul was attacking was cult prostitution and promiscuity and that he knew nothing of stable gay partnerships. It calls for the Bible to be read in the context of its day. On the other hand, it points out that Paul claimed there was no distinction between Jew and Greek, slave and free, male and female (Galatians 3:28), a breathtaking claim in his day. Meanwhile Jesus came to bring good news to the poor, prisoners, disabled, and oppressed (Luke 4:18)—and that has to mean in today's language good news for those who are gay. Some proponents of the liberation view would say that since we are made in the image of God (Genesis 1:27), we should treasure the way we are made, and if he made us gay, he surely did so because he wanted us to be this way.

The strengths of the liberation approach are its concern for justice and for the outsider, and its emphasis that Christianity must be *good news*. Its weakness is its overdependence on social-scientific research, its disdain for some of the traditional sources of Christian wisdom, and its naive faith in the harmony of a society based on conflicting rights.

Underlying the liberation approach is, I suspect, a deep sense that the world of the Bible is a very different world from the one we live in today, and an honest attempt to place the church in the vanguard of the progressive forces in society rather than always lagging grumpily behind. It sees freedom as the heart of God's will and purpose for his creation. If the liberation view were left to itself, the nightmare vision would be of a church losing identity, subtly lacking in self-esteem, losing contact with historical Christianity, and lacking a gospel distinct from a secular, liberal agenda. Remembering that those who wed the spirit of the age quickly become widows, the question I would want to ask the liberation proponents is, "Can you demonstrate to the rest of the church that your main concern is to be faithful to the God historically revealed in Christ, rather than simply to take up the fashionable cause of the moment?"

These then are four theological approaches to the issue of homosexuality. I have three purposes in setting them before you. The first is to say that I think they are all legitimate approaches. It is wrong to say one is true to the Bible and the others are not. It is wrong to say one is loving and the others are not. It is wrong to say one is concerned with justice and the others are not. My guess is that while some people will identify wholeheartedly with one of these four approaches, many will want to take the best bits from all four. (That might be called the Anglican way.) It might be worth saying that I can think of gay Christians who would recognize themselves under each of these four approaches. The second thing I want to say is that all four views are represented in most congregations. I see that as something to be proud of, not to apologize for. I am proud of it. I believe the very existence of churches where all four views are respected is good news.

The third and last thing is this. We could settle for a polite tolerance, all head off into separate congregations with consistent opinions, and never have to meet someone we disagreed with. But we are gathered here this morning, not because we find Christianity helpful or comforting, but because we believe it is *true*. What we have to offer the world is not a book full of answers but a way of continuing a conversation with God and with one another. That way is a way that meets together, recognizes our own sinfulness, shares joy, listens, seeks the truth, prays, seeks reconciliation, gives thanks, shares bread, receives blessing, and thus renews its mission. It is the Eucharistic way, made possible by the truth and reconciliation found in Jesus. We have been given this precious gift in the Anglican Communion, and no denomination is better placed than we are to engage these questions in a spirit of unity and peace. Our gospel is that Christ has broken down the dividing wall of hostility (Ephesians 2:14). If we can't all stay in the room and talk to each other, we're telling the world our gospel isn't true. I'm not sure we can look to the wider church to somehow settle this issue for us. We shall somehow have to settle it for ourselves, and the *way* we do so, in the power of the Spirit, as much as any answer we come to, will be our gospel, the truth we offer to our world today.

Notes

1. Philip Larkin, "Annus Mirabilis," http://www.poemhunter.com/poem/annus-mirabilis/ (accessed June 10, 2008).
2. Tom Wolfe, *I Am Charlotte Simmons: A Novel* (New York: Farrar, Straus and Giroux, 2004), 362–63.